Teaching English
a linguistic approach

Teaching English

a linguistic approach

JOHN KEEN

Methuen & Co Ltd

First published in 1978 *by Methuen & Co Ltd*
11 *New Fetter Lane London* EC4P 4EE
Filmset in 'Monophoto' Ehrhardt 10 *on* 11½ *pt*
and printed in Great Britain by
Richard Clay (The Chaucer Press), Ltd,
Bungay, Suffolk
©1978 *John Keen*

ISBN 0 416 70810 2 (*hardbound*)
ISBN 0 416 70820 X (*paperback*)

Acknowledgement

'In a station of the metro' by Ezra Pound is
reproduced (p. 86) by kind permission of the
publishers, Faber & Faber Ltd.

Contents

Preface

Teachers now have available to them more knowledge than ever before about language and the part that it plays in the learning that goes on – or does not go on – in schools and in colleges. Yet this knowledge is only slowly having an impact upon classroom practice. Teachers too often persevere with teaching methods that don't work, using books that reproduce the same ineffective approaches for generation after generation. The evidence provided by the Adult Literacy Project, which caters successfully for people of all ages from 16 to 87, is proof enough that some of the time-honoured approaches to students' language problems have never worked.

John Keen attempts, in this book, to show how linguistic knowledge of language, that is, scientifically-based knowledge of language as opposed to the mythical knowledge still current in schools and colleges among teachers of all disciplines, may be used to give effective help to students in need of it. He regards it as axiomatic that students in schools and colleges have a right to effective help from their teachers. It follows from this that teachers have a professional duty to understand how such help can best be given, and this implies, given the knowledge now available, a need to understand the approach advocated here.

This approach is rooted in the belief that *all* students possess some skills in using language, and that, essentially, teaching consists in showing how best they can use those skills, and how best they can improve skills that aren't adequate to meet demands made on them. The need to write appropriately, and at length, in a given context, is a task that is constantly laid upon students. In successive chapters, John Keen deals with aspects of this process – with spelling and grammar, with the notion that writing appropriately is essentially a matter of making 'meaning in context', with the means by which we ensure that what we write becomes a coherent whole.

His message is a simple one: that an adequate knowledge of language is essential to the teacher if students are to get the help to which they have a right. He not only argues his case persuasively, but gives an abundance of examples to demonstrate the practice.

July 1977   *Geoffrey Thornton*

Introduction

Nobody these days doubts the importance of language for education. We have learned in the past couple of decades that the way teachers use language in the classroom has a marked effect on how students and pupils learn. We are becoming gradually more aware that language is important, not only in the English lesson, but also in the other humanities subjects, and in the learning of science and crafts. We are becoming more aware that some children are failing in our schools and colleges when they should not be failing, and that this has something to do with language. 'Language for learning', 'language across the curriculum' have become part of the educational vocabulary. And what goes on in the English lesson is central to all these problems. Yet what does go on in the English lesson? The following chapters are directed to this question. They represent an attempt to work towards an approach that has emerged from my own changing perception of what English teaching is.

The question that underlies each chapter is this: what are the best ways of using the language skills already possessed by students and pupils? (I shall hereinafter refer simply to 'students'.) Answering these questions in a practical way means asking many others en route. How can we describe and assess 'language skills' and what access do we have to them? Is it possible to achieve this aim, or would it be better to discard existing language skills and replace them with something else? People working in the study of language have provided the means for a response to these questions. This book is such a response.

What I say makes few claims to originality. It is much more a synthesis of what is already known, and my aim is to make this knowledge more accessible to teachers. If this book stimulates some interest in this relatively unfamiliar material by showing its relevance to the classroom then I will count it as a success.

I would like to express my thanks to Geoffrey Thornton for his help and encouragement, to Dr Avis Dickinson for her patient support and to my students who have taught me as much as I have taught them.

1 Structures and functions

Structures

People can speak and understand the speech of others; it is hard not to feel awe at that, for what lies behind speaking and understanding is the most complex system made by man. The complexity is coded in the mind of each speaker, yet it remains, for the most part, unexploited in schools and colleges. People in education tend to take for granted what students know already, and to focus on what they do not know. This is a dangerous policy for it produces a mean caricature of education; if we are to have an attitude of humility towards what we do not know may we not also glory in what we do know? It is dangerous also because it is inefficient. To learn something it is necessary to be able to fasten on to it by already acquired knowledge and skills. Without this process new knowledge would merely be stored without being assimilated.

In language study there is a unique opportunity to translate this theory into meaningful educational practice. All speakers have a profound familiarity with the language they speak. This familiarity is implicit rather than explicit; a speaker of English 'knows' the grammatical rules which allow him to say, 'It's a great big fat red thing.' but not, *'It's a red big fat great thing.' (* indicates a sentence which is unacceptable in a language.) But that does not mean he could *say* what the rules are. The question is, how can the implicit knowledge of these rules be used? This book tries to explore some ways of answering that question. The place to begin this exploration is with language used by students, and for that purpose I shall discuss the following essay, written by a student early in an 'O' level course.

Market Day in Winter

Bad weather never prevents market folk from doing business. It was a cold day and the snow was falling rapidly. Heavey traffic on the road caused the snow on the road to go slushy. Shop roofs were caped with an inch or more of snow. Snow clung to the glass of
5 windows and reminded me of views on christmas cards.

People walked quickly round the stalls of the market and only stopping to buy goods and not to look. Children in prams cried because they were cold and getting wetter by the minute. Water from snow flowed off the canvas of the stalls roof to collect in
10 puddles. However the market folk did'nt seem to mind the bad weather. They exhibited their goods with magnificent gestures and had mock arguments to draw attention to themselves.

The stalls were packed with every kind of fruits and vegetables on could think off, but the bad weather did nothing to highlight
15 their grandness. Another stall was packed with antiques but trade was slow as bargin hunters were few and far between.

The hat and glove stall was doing a tremendous trade, has many shopers did not anticape the wintery weather the afternoon brought.
20 At the bus stop dozens of people queued for buses that had been delayed. The queues of people resembled walls, they were all tighly packed together dressed in long overcoats and each holding an umbrella.

Building in the distance became faint due to the heavy snow fall
25 and only their outlines could be seen. People walking up the streets resembled dark objects without any real shape.

Adults were not amused by the weather but for a short time children playing did received some excitement from the snowball fights, which were going on in the park, adjcent to the market
30 place.

The essay contains several errors of spelling and grammar of the type often marked by teachers 'careless'. This kind of semi-moral judgement is often used because a teacher does not fully understand the nature of an error. To understand an error as representing what a student cannot do it is necessary to understand what he can do, so let us look at this.

Before I begin this part of the discussion I need a generally understood method for bringing out the structure of sentences and phrases; I need a means of grammatical description. In giving a (simplified) set of categories for such a description I shall define the categories by *distribution*. That is to say, classes of words are defined according to the position in which they occur in a sentence. Words which occur in the same kind of position will count as members of the same class. So, for example, the occurrence of 'the' or 'a' in a sentence signals the fact that at some later point a *noun* will occur. So a definition of 'noun' might include the characterization, 'a non-adjective occurring after "the" or "a".' (This assumes we have already defined 'adjective'.) There are a lot of problems in defining classes of words this way, but it is a much more accurate method than the 'notional methods', which involve defining classes of words in terms of their general meaning. Thus, 'a noun is a naming word', 'a verb is a doing word'. These definitions work perfectly well for someone who can already differentiate nouns and verbs, but they are no use to anyone else. For example, does not the word 'run' in 'Run to the shop' name the act of running? And is not 'movement' a doing word *par excellence*? For more detailed discussion I would refer the reader to any of the introductory books on grammar mentioned in 'Further Reading' at the end of this book. My proposed classes of words are:

N (*Noun*) Any word which can occur in the context (T) – V
      Any non-adjective occurring after 'the' or 'a/an'
      Any non-adjective occurring after an adjective

V (*Verb*) Any word which can occur with a past tense marker (often -ed)
      Any word which can occur with -ing

A (*Adjective*) Any word which can occur between 'the' or 'a/an' and N but not before plural -s

T (*Determiner*) Any word which can occur before N or A but not before V

P (*Preposition*) This class of words is small enough to be defined initially by listing ('in, on, to, with . . .')

wh- (*Relative pronoun*) Any of the following words occurring between N and V: which, who, that, what, where, when.

These definitions are based on Harris (1946). They are not intended
to be watertight; they are intended to suggest the lines on which a
full characterization might be done. Again I urge the reader to more
specialized works to fill in the gaps.

Let us look first at the student's noun phrases. These are sometimes
of great complexity. I shall list the structures he uses, with examples
of each:

(1) N *or* T N

business (line 1)	their grandness (line 15)
the snow (line 2)	an umbrella (line 23)

(2) A N *or* T A N

bad weather (line 1)	a cold day (line 2)
magnificent gestures (line 11)	the bad weather (line 14)

(3) N N *or* T N N (The first noun modifies the second).

shop roofs (line 3)	christmas cards (line 5)
the bus stop (line 20)	the snowball fights
	(= T(N N)N) lines 28–9)

(4) A N P T N

heavey traffic on the road (lines 2–3)

(5) T N P N

the glass of windows (lines 4–5)

(6) N P N N

views on christmas cards (line 5)

(7) T N P T N

the stalls of the market (line 6)

(8) N wh- V (V stands for the whole of the complex verb; here
'had been delayed').

buses that had been delayed (lines 20–1)

(9) T(N N)N wh- V P T N P T N N

the snowball fights which were going on in the park adjcent to
the market place (lines 28–30)

(I am counting 'adjacent to' as a preposition, even though it is not a single word, because single-word prepositions can substitute for it. e.g. 'the park *near* the market place').

All human beings in the process of learning how to use language have to feel their way experimentally towards its rules. In the light of the above data it would not be implausible to suggest that this student is experimenting with the English noun phrase. Linguistic analysis alone cannot give us a direction for teaching; but when this analysis is coupled with a statement of principle a direction for practice can follow. In this case, for example, believing that we should 'start where the student is at' tells us nothing about what we can actually *do*. And merely having some tools for linguistic analysis gives us no clues about what to do with them. To adapt Kant, principles without methods are empty; methods without principles are blind. With both, however, we can begin to develop useful lines for classroom practice. For example, the student has included several NN constructions. These are particularly interesting to teachers and students who are concerned with exploring language, since even a brief examination of them brings out the enormous complexities that are concealed by seemingly simple constructions. Here is a possible lesson guide for such an exploration:

Session 1

The NN phrases used in the essay should be listed and used as a core for obtaining a larger set of NN phrases. This may be done by asking the class for words that can fill the gaps created by deleting a word from each of the NN phrases. Thus:

> Fill each blank with a noun:
> bus —   — stop

(If students are unfamiliar with the term 'noun', or find that they are not sure what counts as a noun and what does not, the teacher might introduce a simple test, stipulating that each word suggested for the blanks should also be able to fit in 'It's a/an —'. So 'company' and 'door' would pass the test, whereas 'large' would not.) The resulting phrases might include ones similar to these:

bus —	— stop
bus company	emergency stop

bus driver	door stop
bus shelter	pit stop

As many phrases as possible should be collected.

Session 2

The data obtained from session 1 should be displayed. The class should be asked to restate each phrase in some other way, keeping the original meaning. This might result in something like:

The driver of the bus *or* The man who drives the bus

A shelter for bus passengers

A stop because of an emergency

A stop for the door

A stop at the pit

Already it is clear that the seemingly simple NN construction subsumes a large number of other different constructions. If the class wished to take the exploration further they could group together forms that they perceive to be similar in structure. Or they could examine other apparently similar structures which cannot be expressed as NN phrases. For example, 'a stop for the door' can become 'a door stop', while 'a present for my mother' cannot become 'a mother present'. (The rules which constrain NN phrases are not absolute, and there is a good deal of room for creativity; it may be more useful to talk of rules and tendencies rather than just of rules. In poetry particularly 'a mother present' could be used as a legitimate construction. Dylan Thomas, one of the more ingenious exploiters of English grammatical rules, refers, in 'After the Funeral', to 'a judgment clout' and a 'fountain heart', both of which are NN phrases which would be thought deviant, or at least odd, in ordinary speech.)

One of the values of the kind of exercise outlined is that it has an explicating function; the skills which the student showed in his essay have been made explicit. This in itself may be counter-productive, of course. One criterion we have for judging skilfulness is how well a person can perform a task without thinking about how he is performing it. But in this case the explicitness of the skills means that the student is more aware of the choices available to him, and it is partly in this that the process of widening the possibilities of language use consists.

It is important to recognize that 'explicitness' is not an absolute idea. Books on formal grammar try to achieve maximum explicitness by means of careful enumeration of relevant categories and painstaking descriptions of how these categories interact. Most speakers of a language could describe very few of the rules of their language in this explicit way; for them language is to be used, not to be studied. Yet between these two extremes there is a spectrum. Knowing how to construct the sentence, 'People walked round the stalls' requires only an implicit knowledge of grammatical rules. Knowing that these two sentences have the same structure requires more than just implicit knowledge:

| People | walked round | the stalls. |
| The water | flowed off | the canvas. |

And knowing that 'people' and 'water' are nouns, and belong to the same class of words as 'wheelbarrow' and 'dichotomy' involves a yet more explicit knowledge of language rules. The level of explicitness which we may use with our students depends on the level of explicitness they have already achieved and on the structure we wish to make clear. There is no point using a fully explicit grammatical description if the point can be made by a comparison with a similar structure. For example, if a student writes a 'sentence' like:

*People queueing for buses.

and a teacher wants the student to see that he ought to have used a finite form of the verb, then the teacher can either say, 'You should have used a finite verb' or he can compare this structure to ones in which the student has used a finite form, and take that as a point of departure. Thus:

*People queueing for buses.
People walked round the stalls.
Water flowed off the canvas.

This procedure involves a relatively low-level explicitness which consists of the act of comparing the structures rather than of describing them.

The same argument and principles that applied to the student's

NN phrases may be applied to the student's use of verb constructions. One of his favourite constructions is NV(N)P(T)N. (Items in
brackets are optional.)

N	V	(N)	P	(T) N
People	walked		round	the stalls. (line 6)
water	flowed		off	the canvas. (lines 8–9)
they . . .	exhibited	their goods	with	gestures. (line 11)
people	queued		for	buses. (line 20)
they	were dressed		in	overcoats. (lines 21–2)
Adults	were not amused		by	the weather. (line 27)
children	received	excitement	from	the fights. (lines 28–9)

(I have counted verb particles as prepositions to simplify the
analysis.)

When we are trying to understand someone's mistakes we need to be
able to place them in the context of correct performances. Indeed one
cannot make a mistake in something unless one can do it fairly well
to begin with. I can make a mistake in speaking French because I can
speak a little French. I cannot make a mistake in speaking Hindi
because I can speak no Hindi at all. If this seems obvious and trivial,
consider the approach to teaching that concerns itself with students'
mistakes out of the context of things the student can do well. The
student whose work we are considering can use prepositions correctly; indeed he takes a certain delight in using a wide variety of
them, in both noun and verb constructions. Use of the sessions outlined above, or some similar sessions with the NV(N)PN sentences
as a basis, would imply a recognition of that fact – a recognition that
has much more point than the usual kind of encouragement given by
teachers: 'good work', 'a fair effort' and so on. If we look at this
student's mistakes we see that, for example, he duplicates the past
tense in line 28:

Children playing *did received* some excitement . . .

A student at this level of language ability would probably see the
nature of his mistake if it was pointed out to him, but if he did not
then in his text there are similar patternings which may be used to
show him the grammatical choices open to him. The similarity may
be demonstrated simply by placing the two structures together:

Children playing	did receiv*ed*	some excitement. (line 28)
People walking up the streets	resembl*ed*	dark objects. (lines 25–6)
Children playing	*did* received some excitement. (line 28)	
Many shopers	*did* not anticape the wintery weather. (lines 17–18)	

All speakers of a language have an awareness of its grammatical rules. I must stress again that this awareness is present in the way a speaker is constrained by the rules in forming his utterances. It is not normally present in a speaker's ability to state the rules explicitly. With guidance, however, a speaker can achieve explicitness to the extent that he can judge two (or more) utterances to have the same or a similar structure. It is a speaker's ability to use his grammar's rules rather than his ability to state the rules that is exploited in the simple technique outlined here. So if – and I stress *if* – a teacher decides to use a policy of intervention, it begins with the premise, 'Here is something you can do' rather than 'Here is something you cannot do.'

The same approach can be used with profit at the level of the student's spelling. In many cases the student uses the correct form of a mis-spelt word in the essay. Compare:

every kind one could think *off* (lines 13–14)

water flowed *off* the canvas *of* the stalls roof. (lines 8–9)

heavey traffic . . . (line 2)

the *heavy* snowfall . . . (line 24)

has many shopers did not . . . (line 17)

as bargin hunters . . . (line 16)

This is the kind of error we are tempted to call careless. Insofar as this implies that the turpitude is all on the part of the student it is inappropriate. In fact this kind of mistake is often a function of the relationship between the student and the school. Bearing in mind that all the mistakes we have seen so far have been made by a student who knew the correct form, consider this point made by Doughty and Doughty (1974):

Many teachers expect pupils to 'get it down' clearly and acceptably the first time of asking, and to express themselves in 'simple, logical English', without realizing what an extraordinarily complex business this has been shown to be.

And Geoffrey Thornton (1974) expresses the values underlying these assumptions:

> . . . those who guess quickest find the most favour.

In fact this student was aware of the basis for the correct forms of most of the sequences he got wrong. He mis-spells 'tightly' as 'tighly' (line 22) but correctly produces 'rapidly' (line 2) and 'quickly' (line 6). He gets 'shoppers' wrong, spelling it 'shopers' (line 18), but he correctly doubles the consonant before a vowel-initial suffix in 'stopping' (line 7), 'wetter' (line 8) and 'getting' (line 8). Of the rest, 'bargin' (line 16) is normally pronounced 'bargin', and the alphabetical sequence 'ai' is rarely pronounced as short 'i'. 'Anticipate' (see line 18) and 'adjacent' (see line 29) are unlikely to occur frequently in the student's speech so the only clue he has is the orthographic shape – 'the look of the thing' – and he approximates pretty well to that.

The student has made a fairly good job of the task given to him. In other words, he has done what was expected of him. But this is not to say that the project as a whole is educationally unquestionable. A school or college is a society, and societies are made up of messages. This essay is a message which is a response to a message issued by the teacher. The message reads something like this:

> The teacher decides what the student will do.
>
> The student, who is not consulted, adapts to it.
>
> The teacher corrects the student's work because he is an expert.
>
> The student accepts correction because he is ignorant.
>
> The teacher, from past teaching experience, expects a 'descriptive essay', involving snow, colourful scenes and bustling movement.
>
> The student supplies it.

In submitting to this relationship both parties come to depend on it, because assertions like, 'I am a student' and 'I am a teacher' are not just labels but anticipations. I referred earlier to the coupling of a linguistic approach to English teaching with a recognition of the student's concrete situation as a starting-point for language education. The implications of this go far beyond what I have said, and what I will say; but they also include it.

A fundamental principle of a linguistic approach to language is incompatible with the approach currently adopted by English teachers in this country. Lyons (1968) states firmly that:

> The linguist's first task is to *describe* the way people actually speak, not to *prescribe* how they ought to speak and write.

Teachers, unlike linguists, cannot avoid being prescriptive some of the time. But, like linguists, our first task is to understand what speakers and writers *do*. That is the only rational basis for showing students what they *should* do. I want to show, in the course of this book, some of the implications this has for classroom practice.

Functions

The teacher who set the essay I have been discussing and the student who wrote it approached the study of language. The possibilities exist even in this restricted form of communication for understanding and widening uses of language. I have discussed some of the grammatical possibilities, and there are many others. But this study is not entered upon in most English classrooms. Indeed there is rarely any intention to explore language from the start – the nature of the task ensures that. And by 'the nature of the task' I mean the uses to which it could be put. Why might a sixteen-year-old need to describe a market-place? Here are some possible reasons:

> A friend who has never been to one might be curious about what it is like.
>
> The student may have been particularly impressed by the experience and may want to share it with someone.
>
> He may want to make conversation with someone, and this provides a suitable topic.
>
> An acquaintance may be afraid of crowds, and may need reassuring that it is a pleasant experience.
>
> He may have witnessed an accident, and a description of the market place is required by the authorities.

In each case he either wants or needs to describe the market-place. For each case he will select details and style differently. For the first he will be general; for the fifth he will be detailed. For the second he will be poetic; for the fifth, prosaic. But when he is writing a 'descriptive essay' the form and content is not determined by the needs of a concrete situation but by a wholly artificial and largely arbitrary set of constraints. Meaning implies choice, and he has little choice. It is not that a linguistic approach to English teaching has no place for poetic language. It is just that this is not where the approach starts. It starts with the fact that this student – and every other speaker of a language – uses language to do a whole variety of jobs. Wittgenstein (1935), in a famous passage, points to something of this variety: '. . . the term 'language-game' is meant to bring into prominence the fact that the *speaking* of a language is part of an activity . . .'

Review the multiplicity of language-games in the following examples, and in others:

Giving orders, and obeying them –

Describing the appearance of an object or giving its measurements –

Constructing an object from a description (a drawing) –

Reporting an event –

Speculating about an event –

Forming and testing a hypothesis –

Presenting the results of an experiment in tables and diagrams –

Making up a story; and reading it –

Play-acting –

Singing catches –

Making a joke; telling it –

Solving a problem in practical arithmetic –

Translating from one language into another –

Asking, thanking, cursing, greeting, praying.

The dashes after each example remind us that language does not only connect on to itself – it is 'part of an activity'. The writing of 'Market Day in Winter' was not part of an activity; it was a linguistic doodle. And as Wittgenstein remarks later in the *Philosophical Investigations*, 'A wheel that can be turned though nothing else moves with it, is not part of the mechanism.'

Why was the student asked to write the essay? And why did he respond unquestioningly by writing it? The setting of essays is part of the tradition of education, and it has behind it the force of power-ful social and psychological models. One such is the 'disciplines' model: language development is separate from other types of learn-ing. Because learning must be under the control of the educators, language development must take place in the classroom, and only there. So it must have delimited periods of time allocated to it. This period of time becomes institutionalized. It becomes 'the period'. It is taken to be a given in relation to which tasks are seen. And since most real uses of language involve either more or less time than the period allows for, some language task which will fit in with the period must be designed. Then the model of language development as a linear step-by-step process is invoked. Each 'period' is a unit and that unit must be translated into a step. So the unit of time must be made to correspond to a unit of achievement. These are the design specifications of the task, and the essay fulfils them to a thou. So the task becomes standardized; this implies that the task must be uniform so that the fulfilled tasks may be compared and graded. The standard, pre-packaged task – of which the English essay is a classic example – is a *requirement* for an educational structure that takes comparative grading as a major premise.

If time is the first parameter of the educational task, space is the second. The way we organize ourselves in relation to other people and to things that are important to us has great expressive value. A classroom is not just a physical space – it is at the same time a social space. Rows and ranks of desks arranged to face the teacher and nobody else implies a control model of learning. A classroom into which a student may not bring the things that can personalize the space for him implies a social situation. The essay is a response to that situation.

The relationship of control determines the things that are to count as part of the situation. Imagine a teacher who brings a collection of textbooks into a classroom where some of the students are reading *Jackie* or *Valentine*. If they do not put their comics away, they will be asked or instructed to do so. The comics stop being part of the situation, and their place is taken by the books. In the same way, most of the students' language resources are put into brackets in the classroom. The classroom is a place

where you have to use technical terms:

Find me an example of alliteration.

where you present yourself for judgement:

Careless work.

where you have to give reasons for views you take for granted:

Say which poem you prefer. Give reasons for your choice.

All these things enter into everyday language situations, but they are determined by the needs of the situation. If you want to de-coke your motor bike you had better understand what a gasket is. If you are being interviewed for a job you had better not say anything silly. If your father wants you in at ten and you want to stay out till twelve you are going to need good reasons. In the classroom your language is not determined so much by the concrete needs of doing something that makes a difference as by the arbitrary whim of the teacher.

One way in which the teacher can ensure that the scope of a task remains under his control is by constructing a task which is artificial and arbitrary. C. W. Gillam (1960) in *Graded English Language Papers for General Certificate* (*Ordinary Level*) advises us that

> ... it is wise to avoid slang, colloquialisms, rambling sentences, sentences without verbs, and any odd effects ... about six hundred words, in five or more paragraphs, would be a satisfactory average.

In real language the length of a piece of writing is determined by all sorts of factors connected to the needs of the situation, such as the need not to sound peremptory or the need to write a specified number of column inches. It is not usually determined by whim. If a complicated and unfamiliar idea is being thought through then a rambling sentence may be just what is needed. If a particular impression is to be made, a verbless sentence might be very useful, as might a colloquial or a slang phrase. These things are part of the language of most students – indeed of most people. What people need to learn are the situations in which these things are useful or counterproductive, appropriate or inappropriate. If all they learn is that these things are *bad* they have learned nothing, except perhaps another linguistic prejudice.

An example

Some of the effects of asking students to perform language tasks which have no clear communicative functions may be seen in a paragraph from another student's essay. If someone asked me to describe a fairground at night, my first reaction would be, 'Why do you want to know?' My answer to the request would depend on the answer to my question. The question 'Why?' was evidently not one which this student asked her teacher, and no doubt the teacher would have been extremely surprised had it been asked. Yet it is a fair question, and if we do not allow students to ask it we cannot complain if their writing exhibits none of the care and thought we might reasonably expect in a real communication.

(From) *A Fairground at Night*

Finally the fair arrived in our town. I decided to go on the very first night. At last the day arrived, as usual I went to school, but the day seemed to drag. The evening soon came quickly. I was going on my own, which I thought was alot better than going with the family or a friend. As I approached the common I smelt the typical fairground smell, of hot dogs, hamburgers, onions, toffee apple, and candy floss. I could hardly wait to enter. Quickly I paid my admission fee, the bright lights suddenly hit me, my eyes were dazzled and the music pierced my ear drums. There were many side shows, amusement arcades, machinary which ran most of the big amusement such as the big wheel, big dipper and flying saucers.

Firstly, note that this is a 'typical' fairground; it is a vague abstraction from dimly remembered experiences of actual, particular fairgrounds. The student has been presented with a functionally ambiguous language task. A description of a *typical* fairground would not have been written, or spoken, as if the writer were present. And a description of an actual fairground would probably be based on a recent experience – an experience that is by its nature transient. The student is being asked to provide both kinds of description at once. And she fails because she cannot handle the two hopelessly confused language functions at once.

The precise ways in which she fails are instructive. She makes two contradictory statements, one next to the other:

. . . the day seemed to drag. The evening soon came quickly.

Why, as she was writing, did this student not see the contradiction? I suspect it is because she was working from a recipe: something like, 'Describe your thoughts and feelings as well as the events.' So she dutifully relates some 'thoughts and feelings' of the kind that English teachers seem to like. Unfortunately, in her desire to invent some feelings that will make her teacher happy she trips herself up and writes down two sets, which happen to contradict each other. There is no reality to these feelings; they exist only in the rules that determine what mark you get for your essays. Yet the student is responding as best she can to a task that forces her to respond with bewilderment and dishonesty.

The same considerations motivate her list of 'typical fairground' smells. Toffee apples do not have much of a smell, and what they do would certainly be masked by onions and hamburgers. Again, this list is to do with the typical fairground, yet the rules of the game insist that the student write her essay as if it were a particular, experienced fairground.

This sense of unreality is present throughout the passage. Her entrance into the fairground is written as if by a passive recipient of events. One moment she is outside, then she is inside; no queueing, no fiddling for change, no walking through. The task is to write an essay, not to say something real, so irrelevancies, like what actually happens, must be glossed over so that the creative writing can start. The student says, 'I could hardly wait to enter'. She means, 'My teacher can hardly wait for me to enter into some poetic prose'. And this student knows what 'creative writing' is. She can use the right kind of vocabulary: 'bright . . . dazzled'; metaphors: 'the bright lights hit me', 'the music pierced my ear drums'. But by the next sentence her perceptual faculties have completely recovered, so that she can observe in great detail the items that constitute the fairground. In reality, of course, people take some time to adjust to being dazzled and having their ear-drums 'pierced', but this is not reality. Again, the switch is from an actual, particular experience to an abstract, archetypal fairground, and the incongruity of the transition does not occur to the student, just as it did not occur to the teacher who set the essay.

Two reasons why teachers find it so hard to detach themselves from the apparent inevitability of the essay are, firstly, that it conforms to their conception of the relation between thought and language, and secondly because their educational experience provides them with no alternatives. The model of the language–thought relation is reflected in instructions and comments, and in the nature of the task. Mr Gillam (in *Graded English Language Papers*) tells us to

Arrange your ideas under five or six main headings ... read as much good English as you can in order to ... gain knowledge and ideas for composition.

Teachers tell us:

You must organize your ideas before writing them down.

Good ideas – poor expression.

Think before you write.

The model is simple: you have an idea, then you express it in words. Ideas cause words. And the nature of the task reflects the same model. A classroom is a room stripped of the furniture of everyday social interaction. There are no objects or events that need to be described or reported. Letters written for exercises will never see the inside of an envelope. Conversation is sometimes prohibited, or discouraged. Nobody needs to be persuaded of anything, because it does not matter if they are not. There is nothing real for language to latch on to, so it must latch on to something unreal, and all that is left for the source of classroom language is 'ideas'.

This model is very clearly at work in 'A Fairground at Night'. The writer was expected to write on the basis of some 'pictures in her head'. Unhappily for this approach pictures in the head are not like real pictures; you cannot examine them closely, and they are only accessible to one person at a time, so they can not be talked about by others.

The model has been refuted time and time again by philosophers, psychologists and linguists. I shall not duplicate the arguments. Instead I present a telling simile of Jean-Paul Sartre's: 'Desire is expressed by the caress as thought is by language.'

Desire may exist apart from the caress, as thought may exist in images, memories, vague intuitions. Desire may be stimulated or brought into being by the act of caressing, just as thought may be stimulated by speaking. Desire may be discovered in the giving of a caress, just as an idea may be thought as it is being spoken or written. The real criterion for judging thought is whether our linguistic or physical response to a situation is appropriate. We may set against the 'essay' model the linguistic model:

The essay model

The function of language is to express ideas.

The linguistic model

The functions of language are to persuade, to report, to express, to judge, to move *and so on*.

The linguistic model stresses that all language is valid. It means that the student may bring into the classroom *any* part of his language resources, not just the bits that pass the teacher's tests.

2 Understanding your students' language

'Correctness'

It is perfectly possible to apply a linguistic approach to teaching by picking out techniques and ideas from the work of linguists and using them eclectically. It must be said, however, that a linguistic approach can be unified and coherent. That is, it is possible to combine pedagogy and linguistics at every level of learning and teaching. A good deal of this book is concerned with a linguistic approach at the level of classroom interaction. But the approach is also relevant at other levels, and in this chapter I will suggest that it is relevant in stages which are preparatory to teaching. 'Preparatory' is perhaps misleading because it suggests that the process can at some point be over and done with. In fact a lesson in, say, the penultimate week of term could show the teacher something about the language abilities of his students, and he may use what he has learned in a lesson during the final week of term. 'Preparing' is an ongoing process. By 'preparing' I mean using what students say and write, not as specimens to be assessed, but as clues about the language experience of the students. 'Using' these discoveries could mean basing a whole lesson on them, or simply bearing them in mind.

What can be discovered depends on what you can bring to the language that is used in your classroom. If you believe, for example, that the language of your students is restricted beyond redemption you are unlikely to gain much by listening to it, except a heightened perception of the errors you knew were there anyway. If you believe that the patterns and functions of language of every normal speaker are equally complex and diverse you are more likely to discover features of your students' language which will help you to work out its motivating forces. And if you can further bring an understanding of how language works that goes beyond the rather naive linguistic ideas of English textbooks, you will bring with it a more finely differentiated response to your students' language.

This difference of perspective will make a difference to how, for example, the following utterances are perceived, and what is done with them:

(1) There isn't no milk on the table.
(2) I don't want none.
(3) It wasn't no good.

They are quoted by Peter Trudgill (1975) in *Accent, Dialect and the School* as examples from an American urban dialect. They can also be found in many British dialects. Many people would judge them to be 'wrong' because of the multiple negation, in spite of the fact that multiple negation is used (and is therefore correct) by many groups of speakers. A teacher who could bring to them some understanding of dialects would want to know more about them before he even began to decide what to do with them: is multiple negation restricted to this dialect, or does it occur in others? Would a speaker of the dialect understand, 'It wasn't *any* good'? Do speakers always use multiple negation, or are there situations in which they would not use it? He might relate this feature to the use of multiple negation in Old English, or to the vestiges of it in present day standard English, as, for example, in the constructions 'neither . . . nor', 'not only . . . but'.

The concept of 'grammar' which a teacher uses to judge his students' work will similarly affect how well he can understand his students' language experience. So from one perspective this sentence:

(4) Macclesfield has got discos every night.

would be considered incorrect because 'got' is redundant, and, perhaps, clumsy. A linguistic perspective on this sentence would take its grammar seriously. The verb 'have' to indicate ownership and similar relations is being replaced in English by 'have got', and for very good reasons. Language likes to be patterned, and 'have' in this sense exhibits irregularities:

(5) Have you a cigarette?
(6) ?Have you the cigarettes?
(7) *Have you them?

(7) is quite ungrammatical in my dialect, and is at least odd in most others.

This irregularity, and others like it, is easily resolved by using 'have got':

(8) Have you got a cigarette?
(9) Have you got the cigarettes?
(10) Have you got them?

It is often all too easy for us to decide that a grammatical construction is a mistake merely because it does not match our own grammatical usage. For example, does this sentence contain a grammatical error?

(11) He was sat on the chair for an hour.

It is a construction I never use; I would always say, 'He was sitting on the chair'. But the construction is used by many of my students. I used to try to get them to write, 'He was sitting . . .' until I realized that 'He was sat . . .' involved a thoroughly principled grammatical rule in their dialects. I realized this when I saw these constructions in their writing:

(12) He was stood on the floor.
(13) He was laid on the ground.
(14) He was knelt on a stool.
(All were used in my sense of 'He was . . . ing' not, 'somebody . . . ed him'.)

Sitting, standing, lying (in my students' usage, laying) and kneeling are all verbs involving stationary postures and I found that this construction for the progressive was only used with such verbs. It was never used in this sense with verbs of movement. So, for my students,

(15) He was ran to school.

could only mean that someone ran him to school, and sentences like,

(16) *He was leapt in the air.
(17) *He was climbed the mountain.
(18) *He was dived into the pool.

were completely unacceptable.

The issue here is to do with attitudes. One possible attitude to (11) – my own initial attitude – is that it is evidence of the students' inability to write and speak grammatically; that measured against some standard it is wrong; and that the language system from which it comes is therefore inferior to the system embodied in the 'correct' standard. The opposite of this is the attitude that (11) is just as grammatical as my 'He was sitting . . .', but that my language system differs slightly from that of my students. Every English teacher could multiply examples like this, and what he does with them in the classroom depends on which of the two attitudes he adopts. To broaden the context, I want to argue for the linguistic attitude: when we are comparing two or more language systems we can only ever say that they are different. It is not simply untrue to say that one is superior to the others; it is meaningless. Students will, of course, encounter these attitudes, and they should have opportunities to decide in advance how they will react to them. This is a legitimate concern of language study.

On the face of it, the idea that some forms of language are superior to others is a myth which English teachers have a vested interest in perpetuating. If people start believing that their language is as good as that of their English teachers then they will not need their English teachers. In fact I think the very opposite is true; that it is in the interests of English teachers to help people to understand that their own language is as rich, as complex, as flexible as the language of any other normal speaker. To begin with, people could become proud of their language, and human beings are generally interested in what they are proud of. Secondly the myth of language inferiority is one important factor in the alienation of large social groups of schoolchildren and students from education. For a detailed account of how these mechanisms of alienation work the reader should refer to William Labov's (1969) important paper 'The logic of non-standard English'.

Once these groups become aware of the value of their own language, and aware that their teachers have the same attitude to it, education no longer becomes a process to be automatically resisted. And the third point is to do with sheer educational efficiency. It is the thesis of this book that the development of language ability takes place best when students can relate what they learn to the language experience they have already had. If either student or teacher believe that this experience is invalid or unprofitable then it cannot be the starting-point.

Inadequacy

The belief that the language of some groups of speakers is inadequate is very widespread. It is difficult to refute because there seems to be no single coherent statement of it; it exists as a disconnected series of tacit folklore 'truths' rather than as a body of explicitly stated theory. Much writing on language, from the correspondence columns of local newspapers to the early publications of Professor Basil Bernstein *assume* it. But no work, to my knowledge, tries to *prove* it systematically and exhaustively. I shall therefore set out my own statement of the theory. Inevitably it will be something of a man of straw, but I think it will roughly represent the views of many people, including many English teachers.

Let us call the group whose language is claimed to be inferior Group X and the 'superior' linguistic group Group Y. Then the thesis that X's language is inferior to Y's may be represented by some or all of these statements. (They do not exhaust the possibilities, but I leave it to the reader to think of others.)

(a) X's language is *less beautiful* than ('not as nice as') Y's.
(b) X's language is *less explicit* than Y's.
(c) X's language is *less logical* than Y's.
(d) X's language is *less precise* than Y's.
(e) X's language has *a smaller vocabulary* than Y's.
(f) X's language is *less complex* than Y's.
(g) X's language is *less abstract* than Y's.

Let us take them one at a time.

(a) The difference in how beautiful two things are must consist in some other relevant difference between the two things. It makes no sense to say, 'This picture is exactly the same as that one in every single respect, except that that one is more beautiful'. So the claim made in (a) can only be established by reference to some other difference between X's and Y's language; perhaps Y's language is more complex than X's, and we find complexity a beautiful thing. And judgements about aesthetics are notoriously subjective, so it will be hard to find them a place in a rigorously stated theory.

(b) At once we have a major problem. Does (b) mean that one particular passage written or spoken by an X is less explicit than one from a Y? Or does it mean that the whole repertoire of words and sentences that an X might possibly use is less explicit than the repertoire of a Y? I do not think people usually mean the former. After all, everybody sometimes says things like, 'Pass the thingumyjig'. And if they mean the latter, then enormous problems are raised. For example, the number of sentences available to any language speaker is infinite. (If nothing else you can keep adding '. . . and . . .'). If X's and Y's repertoires are both infinite it is obviously impossible to compare them to see if one is more explicit than the other.

But even if we set this aside problems still remain. If difference of explicitness is to mean anything it must be able to show that (19) is more explicit than (20):

(19) The boys broke the window.
(20) They broke it.

Yet how can we decide without knowing the context which is more explicit? (19), uttered to me by a stranger on a mountainside where neither boys nor windows are visible, would not only be inexplicit, it would be unintelligible. And (20), uttered by a neighbour in the presence of a broken window and a group of fleeing juveniles, or by someone referring to a picture showing such an incident, would be perfectly explicit. Explicitness is a category which only applies to particular uses of language in particular contexts; it makes no sense to apply it to a whole language system.

(c) The first problem is to decide what is meant by 'logical'. Sometimes people refer to a whole language (German, say) as 'logical'. If by this they mean that the constructions are easy to follow then either they have not tried to learn it, or they speak it so well that they have forgotten how complex its rules are.

'Logical' normally refers to the way statements are related to each other. 'If it's wet then it's not dry' is a perfectly logical statement, and 'If it's wet then it's dry' is a perfectly illogical one. Both statements use words and grammatical constructions found in every variety of English. And this has little to do with language because we could easily replace 'If . . . then . . .' by, say, '→' and 'not' by a squiggle '∼', giving, 'It's wet → ∼ it's dry'.

If someone cannot handle logical relations then that proves nothing about his language, only about his ability to think logically. For a discussion of how a speaker of an apparently 'restricted' form of English can use his language system to construct logical argument, see Labov's 'The logic of non-standard English' referred to earlier.

(d) The question of precision is little different from that of explicitness. In making the claim of (d) people may be thinking about the difference between, say,

(21) Fetch me the reel of white tacking cotton which is in the third drawer from the bottom in the white chest-of-drawers.
(22) Fetch me the cotton out of the chest-of-drawers.

Again, these words and grammatical structures exist in any dialect of English. And even if 'tacking cotton' did not exist in Scouse, all that would prove is that Liverpudlians do not do very much sewing.

People might claim that some social groups habitually use a sentence like (22) when the listener needs something like (21) to understand. This is a factual claim, and there may be something in it. But the fact that understanding of this sort is essential for survival in our society makes the suggestion implausible. In any case, speakers have the means for eliciting more and more precise descriptions to any specified level: they can ask. If (22) was used when (21) was needed then the listener can ask 'Which chest-of-drawers?', 'What kind of cotton?'

Precision is sometimes interpreted as 'saying exactly what you mean'. Unhappily for this definition what you mean cannot be separated from what you say. What someone means is an interpretation of, an abstraction from, what he says. Precision in this context is clearly a pretty imprecise notion.

(e) As with all the others, the first difficulty is in deciding what 'a smaller vocabulary' means. What, for example, shall we count as a *word*? Is 'arrange – arranging – arranged – arrangement' one word with four different forms or four different words? Shall we count 'slang' words like 'chick, bird, bint, crumpet' or shall we count them as variations of the one word 'girl'? Shall we count technical terms a speaker uses in his job like 'distribution', 'interquartile' or 'camshaft', 'synchromesh'? Shall we count a word like 'table' whose meaning differs in different contexts – 'dinner table', 'mathematical table', 'water table' – as one word, or as three words, or more? Shall we count a word like 'spineless', which has a literal and a metaphorical meaning, as one word or two? Shall we count all the words a speaker *could* use or just those he *does* use?

And if these difficulties could be overcome somehow, and it was shown that X's vocabulary was smaller than Y's in some meaningful sense, what would this prove? Let us take some examples. Suppose Group Y have the word 'narrator' and group X do not. Is there anything group Y can say that Group X can not? Clearly not. Group Y's

(23) The narrator of *East of Eden* is also the author.

can be expressed by group X as:

(24) The person who tells the story in *East of Eden* is also the author.

Or suppose Group X have the word 'bait' (meaning a packed lunch for taking to work) and Group Y do not. Then Group X's

(25) Have you got my bait ready?

can be expressed by Group Y as:

(26) Have you got my packed lunch for work ready?

The point is that a speaker's strategies for expressing his meanings are not contained only in the number of words at his command. They are contained in his whole language; in his words, in how he combines those words, in how his words and phrases are related at different levels of abstraction and generality. If a dictionary of Group Y's language were twice as thick as a dictionary of Group X's language we could only infer from this that their languages were different, and difference implies nothing about superiority or inferiority.

(f) In most grammatical descriptions of English a distinction is made between 'simple' and 'complex' sentences. For example, a sentence of only one clause:

(27) He gave me a box of chocolates.

is normally described as 'simple', and a sentence with two or more clauses:

(28) He gave me chocolates and I gave him a tie.
(29) When he arrives I'll give him a piece of my mind.

is described as 'complex'. Could we use this distinction to measure differences of complexity between Group X's and Group Y's forms of language? If we found, for example, that 50 per cent of X's sentences were 'simple' and only 10 per cent of Y's were 'simple' would that not prove that X's language was simpler than, and therefore inferior to, Y's? Unfortunately for the theory it would not. To begin with, 'simple' and 'complex' are technical terms in grammar, and they are not the same things as our intuitive notions of simplicity and complexity. So there is nothing simple about

(30) How weary, stale, flat and unprofitable
    Seem to me all the uses of this world!

Yet it is a 'simple' sentence, grammatically speaking.

Secondly, the grammatical distinction of 'simple' and 'complex' sentences ignores other kinds of grammatical complexity. So there is a sense in which

(31) Faintly visible stars were out.

is more complex than

(32) Faint, visible stars were out.

Some grammatical tests can show that 'faintly' depends on the occurrence of 'visible' in (31) in a way that 'faint' does not depend on its occurrence in (32). So if we omit 'visible' in both:

(31a) *Faintly stars were out.
(32a) Faint stars were out.

then (31a) is not grammatical, whereas (32a) is. And in both, 'visible' depends for its occurrence on 'stars', as we can see if we omit 'stars':

(31b) *Faintly visible were out.
(32b) *Faint, visible were out.

If we diagram this information, informally, we can see the difference in complexity:

(31c) Faintly visible stars . . .   (32c) Faint, visible stars . . .

We can say that (31) is more complex than (32) because in (31) 'faintly' is dependent on 'visible', which in its turn is dependent on 'stars', whereas in (32) 'faint' is dependent on 'stars', and 'visible' is *separately* dependent on 'stars'. If we are to compare the relative complexity of two language systems we must be sure that we take every kind of grammatical construction into account and compare like with like. And the fact is that every variety of English has relations of dependency from which sentences and phrases are constructed. Sometimes the kind of complexity present in one language system may be absent in another, but that absence may be compensated for by a different complexity not found in the first system. In these circumstances it simply makes no sense to compare complexity as if it were a unified, absolute property.

I have discussed the claim that some systems are more complex than others at some length, partly because it has achieved some academic respectability. For example, Robinson (1972) supports his claim that 'The Lower Working Class (LWC) use of a less complex grammar . . . suggests . . . a lower degree of efficiency of communication' with some findings of Lawton (1968):

> The way in which use of subordinate clauses is related to class is shown up by Lawton's employment of the Loban Index (Loban, 1963, p. 6) which measures the 'depth' of a clause. Using this index he found that the deeper the clause, the greater the social class difference.

The assumption is that subordinate clauses are somehow more complex than the equivalent means used by LWC speakers to express themselves. This is an unfounded assumption. To take just one point, the rules for which words and phrases can be omitted in a co-ordinate clause (i.e. a clause joined by 'and', 'or', 'but', 'moreover' . . .) are quite as complex. Thus, you can omit the subject in some co-ordinate clauses:

(33) The man cut his arm and the man bruised his leg.
(34) The man cut his arm and bruised his leg.

Is this omission rule less complex than the rule which replaces 'the man' by 'who' in a subordinate clause?

(35) The man (the man cut his arm) bruised his leg.
(36) The man who cut his arm bruised his leg.

Omission of 'the man' in (34) is optional so in that sense (34) is more complex than (36), where the use of 'who' is obligatory. On the other hand, perhaps the kind of 'embedding' shown in (35) is more complex than the 'adding on' of (33), so in that sense (36) is more complex than (34). But there is no difference of complexity in any absolute sense.

(g) The plausibility of this claim, as it is applied to some social groups, rests on observations of limited areas of language. Many grammatical theories distinguish a class of 'abstract' nouns. But just as 'complex' and 'simple' are technical terms, and mean something different to what they mean in everyday speech, so 'abstract' is simply a label in grammar marking out a set of words with particular grammatical properties. For examples, words in this set tend to be suffixed by '-ness', '-hood', '-ity', '-ence' and a few other suffixes. There is a tendency to think that the use of these 'abstract' nouns in language involves more abstract thought than 'concrete' nouns. If this were so, (37) would be more abstract than (38):

(37) There is a difference between equality and sameness.
(38) Being equal and being the same are different.

and since they mean pretty much the same thing there clearly is no difference in levels of abstraction.

There are familiar difficulties in trying to make clear what 'abstract' means. 'Transport' is obviously more abstract than 'car', in some sense. But is 'transcendence' more or less abstract than 'vocalization'? Few things in language study could be more dangerous than taking pieces of language out of context, counting 'abstract' and 'concrete' nouns and drawing conclusions about the relative levels of abstraction of the speakers' language systems. For one thing, different forms of language have different methods for achieving 'abstraction'. One alternative to suffixing by '-ness', '-ity' . . . is to add 'being —'. There are two examples in (38). Another method involves the formula '(*examples*) + "and things" '. So:

(39) Transport in Manchester is very erratic.
(40) Buses and trains and things in Manchester are very erratic.

Unless we understand how a group's language system works our judgement about that system is likely to be very superficial or just plain wrong. We cannot even begin to understand how language systems work until we have adequate linguistic tools to analyse the systems and until we believe that those systems are worth investigating.

The speech of any one speaker may be used as a means for making discoveries about language. Apart from anything else, the language of any one of your students would be worth studying *for its own sake*. Since we all have more than one student, and each student makes his own special demands on us, we cannot afford to do this. But we could, and it would be linguistically worthwhile. This is important because the attitudes of teachers are so fundamental. If the educational process is to be a dialogue it cannot proceed except by mutual respect. A good professional teacher quite validly expects respect from his students. If the students are aware of the value of their language, and they have a right to be so aware, then they may validly expect respect from their teachers.

An example: swearing

To be consistent we must apply these principles even when they seem inappropriate. It has often been suggested to me that one of my functions as an English teacher should be to reduce my students' swearing, on the assumption that it is caused by 'lack of vocabulary'. Now there are many interesting ways swearing can be explored from an objective, linguistic standpoint. For example, Edmund Leach (1964) examines the close phonetic similarity between some 'swear words' and some animal names, like 'fox', 'ass' and 'cock', and he examines similar patternings in other languages.

And on the grammatical level, Quang Phuc Dong (1969), in a parody of some methods used in transformational-generative grammar, demonstrates some grammatical idiosyncracies of some 'swear words'. So, adapting the examples somewhat, we can see that (41) can be expressed by the grammatical structure of (42):

(41) That sleeping child . . .
(42) That child which is sleeping . . .

but that for a small group of words this transformation cannot take place without altering the meaning or making the utterance grammatically unacceptable:

(43) That bloody cat . . .
(44) That goddam cat . . .

cannot become

(45) That cat which is bloody . . . (wrong meaning)
(46) *That cat which is goddam . . .

Another grammatical property of swear words is their ability to split sections of words which cannot otherwise be split. So, both

(47) It's bloody impossible.
(48) It's quite impossible.

exist in most varieties of English, but whereas in some varieties (49) can be used, (50) cannot be used in any variety:

(49) It's im-bloody-possible.
(50) *It's im-quite-possible.

If a linguistic approach seems to be inappropriate to a rational discussion of swear words then we must seek the reasons in our own attitudes. They have nothing to do with language itself; these things are just as accessible to objective investigation as any other language activity.

If I did want to be didactic about swearing I could perhaps suggest to students that there are circumstances in which it is unsuitable. For most students such a suggestion would be unnecessary because they already know when it is and is not appropriate. This topic provides a good example of the way a rational approach to observed language behaviour can provide insights into the general language experience of students. In one of my classes – fourteen first-year engineering students – dirty jokes were used to disrupt lessons. At first I took this to be part of the background noise a teacher must put up with in a 'difficult' class. But noise as such can be anything; they could have shouted football chants or advertising slogans. Instead they told dirty jokes very loudly, then collapsed in paroxysms of mirth. It was not so much that I decided to use these jokes as a lesson focus, it was rather that at times they were the only language materials available.

During one lesson I asked each student who told a joke what situations he felt he was and was not allowed to tell the joke in. I put each answer on the board, and after a while the following schema emerged:

1 *Allowed to tell joke*	2 *Not allowed to tell joke*
In the street	To Mr D— (a teacher)
In the pub	At funerals
In a brothel	To a puff
At work	To old dears
At home	In church
	To the vicar
	To your mother

Column 1 covers peer-group situations, and column 2 other social situations. For these students peer-group interaction and telling dirty jokes were part of the same experience. No doubt a sociologist could have predicted beforehand that they would be. But I am not a sociologist, and what better way of finding out about my students' language is there than simply taking their language seriously? (For a more comprehensive discussion of the relations between peer-group language and other forms of language the reader is referred to William Labov's (1973) essay 'The linguistic consequences of being a lame'.

The class had already explored the structure and functions of football chants; we were able to return to this topic in a later lesson, and explore it in the context of the peer-group, and to discuss how much language contributes to an appreciation of football; the way different kinds of people talk about football, in what situations they talk about it, and what purposes this talk serves. We listened to commentaries on football games and discussed the skills involved in commentating and the way the commentary style influenced the way someone might narrate an incident in a game. We explored the way sports writers presented various games; their styles, their biases and how this style of writing affected the way people talked about football, particularly in their peer-groups. There is nothing very educationally original about this; it is simply that having had borne in upon me the significance to my students of their mates I was able to ask what relation there was between non-peer-group language (commentating, match reports) and the peer-group language of my students. As it turned out, the language they used for talking about football in their peer-groups was pretty heavily influenced by what they heard and read from more formal sources.

Later we used swearing as a focus, and here the influence of social attitudes as a means of instilling into people a sense of their own inferiority was very evident. The class agreed among themselves that swearing was 'not proper', so it was left to me to suggest the possibility that it cannot be entirely unjustified if a lot of people do it a lot of the time.

> *J.K.*: So what's not proper about swearing?
> *Michael*: Well, it's wrong, isn't it?
> *J.K.*: What's wrong with it? Don't you ever do it?
> *Patric*: It's ignorant really. You don't know the right word.
> *Graham*: Yeah. It's only fucking yobboes say 'fucking'.

By examining swearing objectively, by looking at its functions for people who do swear, the class was able to reassess its stereotype of itself. And how can you avoid using language to stereotype others if you cannot avoid using it to stereotype yourself?

The question of stereotyping raises an issue which needs to be taken seriously by English teachers. This is the problem of how useful it is to make explicit features which are implicit in language use. The ability to use the term 'yobbo' to someone is, for better or worse, a language skill, and there is a school of thought which maintains that the primary job of the English teacher is to improve 'language skills'. Some schools of thought conceive 'language skill' much more narrowly than I do when I include the use of 'yobbo' in it. Many conceptions include spelling and grammar (again interpreted very narrowly) and little else. It is possible to teach English without much explicit knowledge of how language works. Children learn to speak by interacting with people who can speak English but who have no formal theories about its structure. It is possible to be taught to read by a teacher who has never read a book about linguistics. The ability to spell and to write sentences will be developed in most students by teachers who have never studied phonology, morphology or syntax. Given motivation and effort on the part of the students and patience on the part of the teacher there is no reason why this process should not continue. How efficiently it is carried out is another matter; it can be and is carried out.

The cracks begin to appear in this monolith as soon as one of the many inter-related conditions for its continued existence ceases to obtain. What happens if a sixteen-year-old student writes like a twelve-year-old because that is the only way he can avoid making mistakes? What happens if a student is so repelled by the ethos of the school that he loses what motivation he had? What happens if he refuses to make any effort? It is easy to talk as if 'basic' writing skills exist in a vacuum, but it is not very realistic. A teacher cannot correct a student's mistakes if the student refuses to make any, and he is not going to write at a sufficiently ambitious level to make mistakes unless he has some grounds for believing that his mistakes (and the things he does well) will be taken seriously. Neither will he write at this level if he believes that what he is writing is not important. It is precisely in these kinds of situation that it is necessary to make explicit what is already implicit in the language behaviour at hand.

The necessity for explicitness is demonstrated in Graham's characterization of himself as a 'fucking yobbo'. We can see this necessity if we see the import of his remark. In making the remark Graham is demonstrating three things:

(1) He demonstrates his skill in using the self-referential properties of language to construct a paradox.
(2) He demonstrates his ability to *use* paradox as a means for making a judgement about himself and his mates.
(3) He demonstrates his apparent low estimation of himself.

The language skill implied by the construction of Graham's remark contradicts the assertion made by the remark. So we have a further paradox; given that paradox construction is not normally the behaviour of a yobbo, if what Graham says is true then it cannot apply to him, even though he implies that he is a yobbo by using the term 'fucking' both as a quoted term and as an ordinary modifier. If Graham's statement is true then it is false. By at the same time implicitly asserting and denying that he is a yobbo Graham characterizes the ambiguity of his position; his self-respect prohibits him from thinking that he is a yobbo, while his awareness of how others describe people who swear – and his tacit acceptance of the values involved – force him, as a matter of logic, to admit that he himself is a yobbo.

Graham and his mates were the kind of students that teachers call 'the thickies' and 'yobboes'. Geoffrey Thornton (1974) points out that students know we refer to them like this. We like to think they do not, but they do. As well as telling me something about his self-perception, Graham's statement also told me that, for him, language used for swearing and language used for categorizing people are connected in a special way. We may guess that his past experience in schools was partly responsible for his self-image. If this were the case, would it be any wonder that he should reject the ethos and values that deny his experience? Since part of our job as teachers is to judge, grade and classify people, we easily forget that the very process of categorization strengthens similarities and differences encoded in the categories, and minimizes features which are irrelevant to those categories, but are far from irrelevant to the people who are being categorized.

The need for explicitness

The necessity to take the language we use in schools and explore it with our students so that we can see the values behind it and the assumptions it rests on is pointed up by the *difficulties* teachers and students experience. When things are going smoothly you do not need to examine your assumptions; when things go wrong you may do. Furthermore, if we leave our language use in schools unexplicated we are in danger of continuing to alienate young people from our schools. John Holt (1972) points out that

> An important part of what makes a tyranny is that its power is *vague*. it has no limits. You can never tell when it will move in on you. What is wrong with imaginary crimes like being un-American, counter-revolutionary or unco-operative in school, is that you can't tell in advance what they mean. You only find out you've done wrong after you've done it.

When you instruct someone to write an essay, you assume that they know what an essay is. But there are dozens of ways of doing it wrong, and not all of these ways are regulated by criteria other than the whim of teachers and examiners. All the following comments made on essays express something of what an essay is supposed to be:

Too short

Confused

Do not use 'you'

Don't underline in essays

Never use 'I suppose' or 'something'

How often will students get a chance to enquire for themselves what their teacher conceives an essay to be? How many teachers could state exhaustively, in advance, all the criteria they in fact use to decide what is to count as a good essay? Of course, this does not just apply to essays. It applies to every language task a student is called on to perform and to reach a certain standard in. If a student is to work efficiently and honestly he needs to know what the requirements of the task are, and one place on the curriculum where this can be done is the English lesson.

Not only must the teacher be aware of his students' thematic language structures, the students must also have opportunities to discover the important language structures and uses of their teachers.

From this enquiry it will be possible to move on to uses of language that are of less obvious and pressing concern to students. Writing business letters, negotiating, making speeches and writing reports are not concerns of weighty moment to most sixteen-year-olds. But they will be, and school is one of the most important places for rehearsing them. For many teachers it is enough that their students can perform the tasks competently. A linguistic approach demands more than just the skills; it demands that the students should understand explicitly what the tasks constitute. Peter Doughty (1973) points out that 'we are creating a society in which the normal state of that society is one of change'. If we simply prepare people to write business letters on the style approved of in the 1970s, the same people may be at a loss if they cannot manage the style in vogue in the 1990s. When we talk about preparing students for work and for society we must remember that these concepts are constantly changing. And the only way to ensure that a student is prepared for the language tasks of a changing society and employment structure is to ensure that he understands how those tasks are conceived by the other people involved in them, and the functions those tasks must perform.

3 Spelling and grammar: some linguistic implications

In this chapter I want to explore some of the contributions that linguistics can make to some of the purely practical problems that are shared by all English teachers. To do this I will follow the method used in other sections and use a corpus of writing by a student as a basis for discussion. Some of what I will say overlaps with some suggestions made in chapter 1, but I hope the reader will find some of the possibilities put forward in this chapter more thoroughly worked through.

Before the practical we must make clear some theoretical points. Language can be understood as operating on several different levels. By judiciously 'putting into brackets' some of our knowledge of language, we can concentrate attention on one aspect at a time. So, for example, we can ignore the fact that a language has rules for ordering words and phrases and that these words and phrases mean something, and we can concentrate on the way a language organizes its sounds – the *phonological system*. Or we can put this in the background and look only at the meaningful units used in the language – the *morphological system*. Or we can take these two systems for granted and look at the rules which order and relate units of meaning – the *grammatical system*. Or we can study the meanings of words and phrases, and how these meanings are related – the *semantic system*.

In fact these systems interact with each other, but each system does have a life of its own, and it is only possible to obtain a clear picture of the very complex relations between the systems if we treat each one as autonomous. Using an actual – and not untypical – piece of writing from a student I want to show how relevant a sound knowledge of the phonological, morphological and grammatical systems can be to a teacher.

My corpus is a short passage written as the copy for a holiday brochure designed to attract young people to come to Macclesfield for their holidays.

Macclesfield – the place to be, it as got discos every night at diffrent places. It as got a good county were you can spend luying in the fields. Get into Manchester which as all the fasions A number of pubs Around Macclesfield they or lacks and rivers were you can go and fish. If your one for boating it is a good place for it. They comes into Macclesfield a fair twice a year this is a big one. They is a bus serves if you have not got a car.

If we consider this passage on the morphological level, and bear in mind the kind of reader for whom it was designed, it has much in its favour. The student refers to discos, good country, fashions, pubs, lakes and rivers for fishing and boating, a fair and a bus service, all of which would no doubt appeal to his intended readers. He opens with a vigorous slogan – 'Macclesfield – the place to be' and uses colloquial idiom to add colour – 'If your one for boating . . .' However, if the passage were to be included in a brochure the reader's reaction to it would probably be quite unfavourable. It is likely to attract ridicule and teachers have a duty to prevent this as far as possible.

Spelling is as much a social invention as a linguistic one. The English language itself is far more tolerant of mis-spellings than are the speakers of English. Spelling 'dependent' as 'dependant', for example, could never produce ambiguity or lack of understanding, yet most people would count it as a spelling mistake. Two questions to which students have a right to know the answers are:

What are people's attitudes to spelling?

What effect does mis-spelling have on the intelligibility of a piece of writing?

Linguistics has well-established methods for answering questions like these. These methods are *empirical*; they try to discover the facts of the situation irrespective of emotional or moral considerations. The answer to the first question may be obtained by the simple expedient of asking people. Of course, the right questions must be asked, but most classes could design some questions that would give them the answers they need.

Questionnaires and interviews are both used by sociolinguists to elicit attitudes to language. Students come into contact with several social groups and age ranges. So there is no reason why they should not discover for themselves what other people's attitudes to spelling are, and their reasons for those attitudes. They might ask some of these questions, for example:

Do you expect official letters to be spelt correctly?

Do you think spelling has anything to do with intelligence?

Do you expect personal letters to be spelt correctly?

Do you think schools should put more emphasis on spelling?

These are perhaps the simplest kinds of elicitation procedures. A more complicated kind would be needed to establish an answer to the second question. If a linguist wanted to find out the limits of variation in a spelling system he might design a test. In this case he might write a dozen or so short sentences and insert spelling mistakes in each one, with the number of mistakes increasing for each sentence. So his test might look like this:

Do you understand what each of these sentences means? Write YES, NO or NOT SURE against each one:

The pencal was near the book.

Yor mony is in this envelope.

Mi ca fel over that clif.

Hiz antie travells buy motor coach.

Ninty peple rote to there councillors.

Thi plain flu accros thi contry.

Or riprisintitive wil cal one yu.

Once we begin to look at this question practically we discover all sorts of complicated issues. What, for example, *is* a spelling mistake?

'Pencal' is clearly a mistake for 'pencil', and 'flu' a mistaken version of 'flew'. But how many spelling mistakes are there in this passage quoted in Carol Burgess *et al.* (1973) *Understanding Children Writing?*

> My happiest moment
>
> And The Thee I was. goos dos Inow get e sis we good D. Party I news siwed The wale masfed it a big dog. and away. Les dud wot.

Can we control in our tests for seriousness of error? 'Pencal' is not a serious error, but 'horse' for 'hoarse' could be in the sentence 'I am a little —'. Are any of these mistakes likely to occur in anybody's writing? Are some more likely than others? These are all reasonable questions, and students have the right to consider them seriously and objectively. There is no reason why a class should not design their own tests on these – or some similar – lines and discover the questions, and perhaps some answers, for themselves. If a class has made some effort to find out about spelling in its relation to intelligibility and about people's attitudes to spelling they may also find that the communicative functions of spelling do not always provide the basis for people's opinions about it. They may also find that more effort and time is needed to read something which is badly spelt. And they may find that sometimes mis-spellings make it impossible to know what a writer meant, but that sometimes they do not. These discoveries are not a substitute for learning to spell; they involve an awareness of the need – or the lack of need – for correct spelling.

This awareness is important for students who are at that stage of language development when they are learning the refinements of spelling. It is necessary to stress that they are learning refinements and not basics. If a student spells 'different' as 'diffrent' he requires only a minor modification, not a fundamental reappraisal, to get it right. Techniques that have been developed in linguistics are useful here too, and an English teacher needs to know how the English spelling system – for a system it is – works in order to exploit these techniques.

As most people know, English spelling is partly phonemic, or based on the *phoneme* as a unit. A phoneme is simply a class of sounds none of which contrast with each other in a language. For example, many Geordies have two 'r' sounds; one ('uvular r' – [R]) is articulated with the back of the tongue against the roof of the mouth, and the other ('alveolar r' – [r]) articulated with the tip of the tongue against the alveolar ridge at the front of the mouth. As *sounds* they are very different, but they never make a difference to the meaning; a Geordie will accept your offer to buy a [R]ound of drinks (though he would not say it like that) with the same alacrity as he will if you offer a [r]ound of drinks. So [R] and [r], plus some other sounds, belong to the same class of sounds, which in this case is, for convenience, called /r/. Of course, some phonemes of English have no one symbol to represent them in the alphabet; the vowel of '*a*bout' and 'cupb*oa*rd', for example. Some phonemes have more than one symbol to represent them; the sound in '*sh*ine' is a single sound, just as 's' is, but it needs both 's' and 'h' to represent it. And some sequences of phonemes are represented by only one letter; the /ks/ in 'e*x*pel', for example. Mostly, these sound–symbol relations are pretty consistent, but sometimes they seem not to be. For a lot of these cases there is a different spelling system alongside the phonemic one; a morphophonemic system. 'Morphophonemic' refers to the interaction between the phonemic and the morphological systems of a language. A *morpheme* is a minimal meaningful element of a language. So 'books' can be analysed into {book-} plus {PLURAL} (here '-s'), but neither {book-} nor {PLURAL} can be analysed further, so they are minimal units, or morphemes. 'Antidisestablishmentarianism' consists of six morphemes, only one of which – {-establish-} – can normally stand by itself as an individual word. Morphophonemics, as the name suggests, is to do with how morphemes are translated into sounds. So /-s/ and /-z/ can both be used to indicate a plural, as in 'hut*s*', 'home*s*', but both sounds are spelt '-s', never '-z'. Because spelling is intended to be seen it is not unreasonable that it should preserve visual relationships at the expense of phonemic relationships. This principle accounts for the fact that '-man-' is always spelt 'man' even though it may be pronounced as in 'a *man* and a woman', or as in 'milk*man*'. There are thousands of examples:

reform – *reform*ation

famous – in*famous*

differ – *differ*ent

(There are exceptions, of course. Compare:

    space – spatial

    argue – argument

    proceed – procedure.)

There are two main implications for teaching here. The first is simply that an understanding of students' spelling errors is made easier once we see that very often the morphophonemic spelling rules are not being applied, or that they are being applied inappropriately.

The second implication is for how we are to apply this understanding to our teaching. There are several possible ways of doing this, but I want to suggest the one I think is the most powerful. This exploits the fact that a word or phrase in a language does not exist in isolation but is related to many other items. One very simple way in which items are related is through *paradigms*. Paradigms are simply lists which can be used to bring out regularities or patternings in language. For example, if I want to bring out the fact that the morpheme {-mean-} is involved in the words 'mean', 'means', 'meaning', 'meant' I could set out the words like this:

mean

I ＿＿ it.

He ＿＿s it.

What's the ＿＿ing of this?

He ＿＿t it.

The setting up of a paradigm in order to bring out a pattern or regularity is a familiar technique in linguistics. For the benefit of the student who has spelling difficulties I think it is invaluable. It is all the more so because the more of a language system that is used for teaching the more likely it is that a student will find something he is sure of to which he can assimilate what he learns.

The same principles are relevant to many other mistakes, for example, 'compearing' for 'comparing', 'dint' for 'didn't'. Let me show the patterning and the paradigms, and give a 'running commentary' to sum up some of the points made so far.

compearing

comparison   (This spelling may be known to the student because the second vowel sound /a/ is regularly represented by the letter 'a' ('cat', 'hammer' . . .).)

comparing   (This spelling is not known to the student, possibly because the second vowel sound /eə/ as in 'air' is often represented by the letters 'ea' ('pear', 'bear' . . .) He can, however, see a connection with 'comparison', which he does know.)

Paradigm

compar-

_____ ison

_____ ing

dint

did

did not   (These spellings may be known by the student, because in normal speech there is no merging together of the adjacent /d/ and /n/ sounds, so there are two separate phonemes for him to represent by letters.)

didn't   (This spelling is not known by the student, possibly because in ordinary fluent speech the word is often pronounced *dint*. He can, however, see a connection with 'did not', which he does know. The omission of the apostrophe is a separate issue.)

Paradigm

didn - t

—— o ——

____ , __

The technique of setting up paradigms can enable a student to correct other spelling errors by allowing him to see regularities that are operating. The writer of the essay quoted on page 38 mis-spells 'has' as 'as'. He already knows the form 'have' so a paradigm set like this:

They *have* got discos.

They *had* got discos.

It *has* got discos.

will enable him to see a regularity where otherwise he might only see the word in isolation. Similarly, he mis-spells 'where' as 'were', but he knows the form 'which'. So a paradigm set like this:

The town *which* has all the fashions . . .

The man *who* has all the answers . . .

Lakes and rivers *where* you can go and fish . . .

will bring out the correlation between 'wh-' words and a particular kind of grammatical structure. 'Lakes' as opposed to 'lacks' belongs to a paradigm involving a rule that a word spelt with the sequence 'vowel + consonant + e' at the end of a word is pronounced with the vowel long or diphthongized (i.e. with the tongue gliding from one position to another). If we use the paradigmatic method for revealing pattern we do not need to use this very high level of generality – it would be wasteful anyway, because a much less general rule can provide us with the pattern we need. This rule is illustrated by the paradigm:

lakes – lacks

shakes – shacks

takes – tacks.

Again, a student's ability to make any one of these distinctions provides a starting point for correction within his own competence.

The use of paradigms is not appropriate to all situations. The paradigms to which 'they' and 'there' belong exhibit no clear orthographic patterning. And the confusion caused by the bewildering realizations in writing of the *sh* sound no doubt contributed to the writer's mis-spelling of 'fasion' as 'fasion'. Consider:

fashion   fascist   fission

passion

ration

Asian (in some pronunciations)

Other methods, like practice, will no doubt be necessary to deal with this sort of problem. Linguistics provides no miracle cures; what it offers is methods for making explicit patterns of language which can be exploited in the service of language development. A teacher's ability to recognize what these patterns are and how they are related demands a reasonable level of linguistic skill. His ability to use this skill to educational advantage requires considerably more knowledge of his students' language. In practical terms it may require him to know (or to be able to find out) whether a student is familiar with the word 'argumentative', in which the stress is on the third vowel 'e', so that the teacher can bring out the relationship with 'argument', which is often spelt as 'argumant'. At the grammatical and semantic levels it will require the teacher to have access to more complex and detailed knowledge about his students' language. And it will require correspondingly more complex and detailed methods for describing that knowledge so that the teacher can bring his students' knowledge to bear on their language performance.

Sometimes patterning in language structures is buried pretty deep, and we are deluded into thinking there is no patterning because we are so familiar with the structures. What could be simpler, for example, than the English construction 'there is/are . . .'? In fact we only have to look at the equivalent construction in other languages to see how idiomatic it is:

French   Il y a (He/it there has . . .)

German   Es gibt (It gives . . .)

The writer of 'Macclesfield – the place to be' uses the construction, quite correctly, as a slot-filler to avoid the awkwardness of

Lakes and rivers are around Macclesfield.

A bus service is in Macclesfield.

And even though he mis-spells 'are' he is aware that 'be' becomes singular or plural ('is' – 'are') according to whether the notional subject ('A bus service', 'Lakes and rivers') is singular or plural. To understand why he mis-spells 'there is' as 'they is' we need to look at their respective patternings. In English the process of *vowel reduction* is very common; this process involves the full quality of a vowel being lost, usually in contexts where it is superfluous to the needs of communication. So a well-used and predictable word like 'and' in 'fish and chips' will only have its full quality if it is being stressed:

I don't just want fish; I want fish *and* chips.

Normally the vowel in 'and' will be the unstressed vowel /ə/ – the first vowel of '*a*bout'. The same thing happens to 'but', where giving the vowel its full quality makes the word strongly emphatic. Normally it is just pronounced /bət/. This process applies to 'there is' and 'there are'. To show this process I will use a phonemic spelling in which

/ə/ represents the sound in about

/7/ represents the sound in sit

/e/ represents the sound in set

/3/ represents the sound in earth

/ɑ/ represents the sound in far

/eə/ represents the sound in there

/e7/ represents the sound in they

/j/ represents the sound in young

/ð/ represents the sound in they

/z/ represents the sound in zoo

/r/ represents the sound in very and run

Vowel reductions in 'there are', 'there is' and 'they are'

there are	there is	they are
/ðeərɑ/	/ðeər7z/	/ðe7jɑ/
/ðeərə/	/ðer7z/	/ðe7jə/
/ðərɑ/	/ðər7z/	/ð3/
/ðərə/	/ðəz/	/ðə/

(This set of reductions applies to the writer of the essay's dialect – mid-Cheshire – but not to all English dialects.)

So when someone writes 'there are . . .' he is trying to relate an orthographic shape, not to some pretty definite string of sounds, but to a whole matrix of relations and correspondences. By adopting strategies which focus on these relations a teacher can help his students to match their experience of the patterns in their spoken language with the more restricted correlates of those patterns in the written form. The problem here is that the writer conflates two forms because of their similarity of orthographic shape and phonemic patterning. So one answer is to base practice on forms that contrast as much as possible. These forms contrast:

/ðe7jə/ – /ðərɑ/

In each vowel position an unreduced vowel contrasts with a reduced vowel, a long vowel contrasts with a short vowel and a stressed vowel contrasts with an unstressed vowel.

Practice might consist of the teacher reading out short sentences involving /ðeʒjə/ or /ðərɑ/ and getting the student to match one or other of the spellings to each utterance. Clearly, for different dialects different contrasts would have to be used.

This may all sound very complicated, but in fact it exploits a pretty elementary knowledge of the English sound system. Once this elementary knowledge is mastered it takes no longer to prepare a practice session like the one suggested than it would take to prepare a conventional spelling test.

This problem needed to be analysed at the grammatical level as well as at the phonological and orthographic level. In explaining the differences between 'your' and 'you're' we would also be exploiting knowledge of English at more than one level. In the same way when we look at the grammar of an utterance or piece of writing we will constantly find ourselves taking into account the writer's meanings. For example:

It as got a good county . . .

could mean (i) that Macclesfield is *in* a good county, or it could mean (ii) that Macclesfield has got good *country*. If he meant (i) then we can again use the technique of exploring grammatical patterns through paradigms. A 'sentence' like this:

Macclesfield has got a good ——.

can stand for a very large number of sentences, with all sorts of words and phrases filling the slot. If we use it as a basis we can generate a series of sentences that are guaranteed to have the same structure as the original. If we vary, say, the first slot we can generate even more. This may seem very obvious, but I think the advantages over other methods of grammatical exploration are very great. The patterns come from the students themselves, so they are working with familiar material. They do not need elaborate layers of technical terminology, much of which has dubious validity anyway. They are working from a corpus of actual material to an awareness of more general rules, which is the direction that language development takes in real life. And this method ensures a large measure of control over variables, which can be altered one at a time. Suppose we have worked through the 'sentence' using this method, also substituting for 'Macclesfield', and we have:

———————— has got a good ————————.

Macclesfield	main street.
My house	view.
Woolworth's	toy counter.

It is easy to see that only some of the nine possible 'sentences' are allowed. 'My house has got a good view' and 'Woolworth's has got a good view' are alright, but 'Woolworth's has got a good main street' is much more dubious. To many students alternatives will present themselves – 'Woolworth's is *in* a good main street', 'Macclesfield has got good gardens'. So we can return to the original sentence, and put it next to some of the alternatives which have emerged from the exploration:

Macclesfield has got a good county.

Macclesfield is in a good county.

Of course, the meanings of the sentences are important for deciding which would more usually be said, but similar methods can be employed for exploring meaning, so we will see that there is an economical continuity of method for discussing and working out structures in language on all levels. If the student had intended to write, 'Macclesfield has got a good *country*' the same kind of methods could be used to bring out the differences between 'a good country' (= nation) and 'good country' (= countryside).

So far we have looked at the possibilities for exploring language of simple paradigms constructed from words or from sentences. Often this is enough, but sometimes it is not. Sometimes other operations will be needed if the exploration is to be fruitful. A whole range of such operations are available once a class becomes used to this way of working. I will give a brief example of some of the possibilities using a sentence from the writer's work. Three of these operations are:

Substitution   It has got good *country*. becomes
                 It has got good *rivers*.

(This is the operation we have used to get paradigms.)

Permutation   . . . lying in the fields *all day*. becomes
                . . . lying *all day* in the fields.

Deletion   . . . lying *all day* in the fields. becomes
             . . . lying in the fields.

If we take the sentences:

It has got good country where you can spend lying in fields.

then by using substitution repeated several times we can derive:

He has got good money which he can spend going to the races.

I have got an hour that I can spend talking on the phone.

By another substitution – a noun phrase for 'where/which/that' – we can get:

It has got good country – good country you can spend lying in the fields.

He has got good money – good money he can spend going to the races.

I have got an hour – an hour I can spend talking on the phone.

Already the first sentence is looking a bit odd. If we now permute the noun phrase so that it appears after 'spend', it looks even more odd:

It has got good country. You can spend good country lying in the fields.

He has got good money. He can spend good money going to the races.

I have got an hour. I can spend an hour talking on the phone.

If necessary, all but the essential structure may be deleted so that the point at issue is isolated for the students:

??You can spend country there.

He can spend money there.

I can spend an hour there.

These methods need not be used exclusively for correcting errors. They can, for example, be used to encourage students to explore different ways of presenting their content. One of the features of this piece of writing is the very general nature of much that is referred to: 'at different *places*', '*good* country', 'a *good place*'. It may be that the writer has, albeit unconsciously, compensated for the particularity of the activities – disco's, pubs, fishing, boating – by describing some facilities in a very general way. Or it may be that his experience of the town and its environs is sufficiently restricted to make his description of some aspects of it vague. Whatever the reasons, the methods suggested might be able to play some part in filling out the general terms with particulars. 'Good', for example, is the highest point of a hierarchy of positively evaluative terms. There are millions of ways of being 'good'. 'Pretty' or 'richly forested' make finer distinctions for the reader because they rule out more than 'good' rules out; 'pretty' rules out 'magnificent'; 'richly forested' rules out 'rolling pastureland'. Using some of the operations described, it might be possible to get the rest of the class to add their own experiences to the attempt to find ways of describing Cheshire, simply by filling the slot in

It has got ——— country.

We have entered the area of meanings, and we must tread carefully here. We must remind ourselves that the test of a piece of writing is how well it does the job it purports to do, not how nearly it matches our expectations of how we would do it. If descriptions of Cheshire like

'pretty country',

'picturesque country',

'magnificent country'

were elicited, there might be a temptation to say that they were 'better' because they were more 'precise' or more 'evocative'. There lingers here something of the English teacher's undifferentiated response to 'descriptive writing'. This writer's piece was not intended as a piece of descriptive writing; it was intended to attract young people to Macclesfield for their holidays, and it may be that these very general words are just what would be required to achieve that aim. It may be as Wittgenstein (1935) suggests: 'Is it even always an advantage to replace an indistinct picture by a sharp one? Isn't the indistinct one often exactly what we need?'

But meanings need a chapter of their own where they can be examined in the depth they deserve.

4 Meanings: a matter of context

Definitions

Traditionally, concern with meanings in schools has been with things on the periphery of students' language systems. In a text book intended for students 'up to and beyond O level' we find dozens of questions like this:

> Define these words: induce, integrated, persists, compounded, subtle . . .

In this chapter I will argue that a concern with meanings in education must transcend the approach implied by this sort of question, and I will suggest other, more principled, approaches to the problems.

What is the point of this kind of question? Presumably one function is to test students' vocabulary. But in doing this it also tests their ability to define. In other areas of life the ability to define is necessary, but the situation is never like this. To begin with, the test we use in everyday situations to find out if someone understands a word is that of *use*: someone knows the meaning of a word if he uses it correctly – it is irrelevant whether he can define it or not. Then there is the question of what we need a definition for. Among the biggest consumers of definitions are scientists, and we may learn from them something of the purposes of definitions. Let us take a real live definition from the mathematician Gauss (1801):

> If a number *a* divides the difference of the two numbers *b* and *c*, then *b* and *c* are said to be *congruent* relative to *a*.

Gauss is saying what he will mean by *congruent*. He needs to do this for several reasons:

(1) In other contexts (e.g. 'congruent triangles') the word is used differently.

(2) Like all mathematicians, he needs his terms to have fixed, unequivocal uses.

(3) The term will be used in proofs, and one of the conventions that enable mathematical proofs to work is that the meaning of all terms used should be known in advance.

It is obvious that the text-book exercise is nothing like this. Nobody can lay down in advance the meaning of a word in language (though the *Académie Française* and some teachers try) because the meaning of a word depends on the tacit assent of a speech community, not on one person's *fiat*. And language gently but inexorably changes, so fixed meanings are always liable to become unfixed. Language has strategies for avoiding ambiguity, but they are not the same strategies as in mathematics. Thus, the word 'get' has several different senses – compare 'I'll get the paper.' to 'I'll get cheated.' More often than not the different uses are disambiguated by the context. Mathematicians prefer to disambiguate by using different symbols and different terms whose meanings are precisely stated before any mathematical operations are done.

Mathematical proofs are only one area where language (or rather, a derivative of language) is used. In other areas the precision of meaning that is a prerequisite for doing mathematics at all is not needed. If I invite a friend for dinner at seven o'clock, I do not mean 'seven o'clock G.M.T. as measured by an atomic clock'.

Not all definitions, even in science, are like this. Some definitions are descriptive rather than stipulative, and their functions are often very different. When, for example, a geologist defines several different kinds of rock as 'sedimentary', he is conveniently summing up in a single term a set of similarities that have been discovered by geological methods. The point of a definition of 'sedimentary' would then be not only to inform someone of the meaning of the word 'sedimentary', but also to give them information about how rocks are formed, and to say that this involves a distinction which is important in the subject.

Again, the vocabulary exercise is not like this. The students are not being asked to base their definitions on perceived similarities that they have directly or indirectly discovered. Nor are they being asked to provide information that may be of some use to somebody. They are being asked to look inside their minds and consult the mental dictionary that textbook writers assume to exist. What linguistic evidence there is – and it is controversial – suggests that the method of storing information about meaning in the brain cannot be realistically described by analogy with a dictionary. For example, most English speakers would be hard put to describe the differences in meaning between 'womanly' and 'feminine' just by using dictionary-type definitions. If we accepted the theory that people carry 'dictionaries in their heads' this would seem to prove that most people don't know the difference between 'womanly' and 'feminine'. But people do know the difference: if they were asked which of these two sentences was the more normal:

(1) Alan's three-year-old daughter is very feminine.
(2) Alan's three-year-old daughter is very womanly.

few people would hesitate in their answer. People can use terms correctly, even when those terms embody very subtle distinctions, and those distinctions are beyond their capacity for explicit definition.

Even if the dictionary analogy were accurate, the 'give-a-definition-of' method of eliciting meaning would not be justified. The compilers of dictionaries do not arrive at their definitions by looking into their own minds. If they want to define a word they collect a large number of sentences in which the word appears, and work out the meaning from those contexts. Of course, they also use work done by earlier lexicographers, and they may use their own intuitions, but the *basic* method is contextual. If a teacher demands the skills of a lexicographer from his students then he ought, to be consistent, to provide them with the lexicographer's tools. If this were done, students would be given a dozen or so sentences (more if necessary) each containing the word in question, and they would be asked to work out how that word was used from those contexts. For some items the number of contexts needed to provide relevant information is quite small. So a very small number of meanings are possible for the Japanese word 'e', given these contexts:

Kore wa   e   desu.

This (*marker*) ——— it is.

(This is a ———.)

Tokonoma ni   wa   e   ga   kakatte imasu.

Alcove   in/at (*marker*) ——— (*marker*) hanging   it is.

(A ——— is hanging in the alcove.)

Watashi wa   e   o   kaite   imasu.

I   (*marker*) ——— (*marker*) painting   I am.

(I am painting a ———.)

And a much larger number of contexts would have been needed for a reader to work out the different uses of the markers 'wa', 'ga' and 'o'. The strategy, however, would be basically the same, involving a matching of common features between contexts.

Much of this is already familiar to teachers through the writings of psychologists of education on concept-learning. It is necessary for my purposes to go beyond this relatively familiar ground to a major assumption on which the educational exploitation of theories of meaning rests. This assumption is shared by many educationalists, for whom Liublinskaya (1957) may act as a spokesman: '. . . the child can master words as signals, which generalize a whole group of similar stimuli by abstracting the essential common feature.'

If we imagine the world as it is through a child's eyes, it is clear that to begin with things do not have any 'essential common features'. There is evidence that humans have some ability to make sense of things from the moment they are born, but to all intents and purposes they experience a world of incessant novelty. This sounds like unverifiable speculation, but we may put the same point in logical terms. The idea of two things having a 'common feature' that is part of the 'essence' of those things involves that feature being already present in each of the two things. But in what sense is, say, 'roundness' *in* both a plate and a flowerpot? Certainly not in the same sense as the flower is in the flowerpot. There is no quality or feature *in* both an orange-box and a flat piece of metal resting on tubular supports, but both may be used to sit on. Language has coded these two objects together because they can both perform the same function, not because they have qualities inside them. And most of the important meanings that language makes available to us have functional rather than 'essential' similarities. But functional similarities do not exist just in the abstract; a kitchen stool and an orange-box only become similar when people use them for similar things. In short; we do not receive meanings passively; we impose meaning on the world by acting on it, as well as by being acted upon by it.

Take the example of a severely subnormal child who cannot speak and who is more or less immobile. It seems as if he has no way of symbolizing, of making external, the experiences he has. Indeed, it might seem nonsensical to talk about him having experiences at all since experience requires that something is brought to the raw perceptions in order that they should make some sort of sense. In fact he does have ways of creating meaning from the experiential material around him; one of these ways is rocking, as any visitor to an E.S.N.(S) school will witness. By rocking backwards and forwards monotonously he ensures that he is not merely receiving regularities that already exist 'outside' himself. Nor is he merely expressing feeling that already exist 'inside' himself. He is creating regularities from his available resources, and using them, first to impose order on his experience through the physical representation to himself of the regularities of which his body is capable; second to discover new experiences, kinaesthetic and emotional, through the original physical representation; and third to discover that an undifferentiated flux of arbitrary sensations may be reduced to an ordered sequence of discrete events that can be experienced for themselves, and for their relations to other events of the same kind. Even under these minimal conditions human beings do not merely abstract meanings from the world – they impose meanings on it.

If we are to develop acceptable strategies for dealing with meanings in the classroom, we had better observe closely and sensitively what people do when they make meanings, because making meanings is an active and creative process. I once met, in a school for severely E.S.N. children, a boy who, for physiological reasons, could not speak. He had been taught to count by raising his fingers one at a time while his teacher said 'one, two, three . . .' He would play this game repeatedly without tiring. Clearly he had far more scope for acting on and learning about the world than one of his non-ambulant companions, but the principle was the same: he could interact with his environment through the resources of his own body. Later, I was told a story about him: he had been taken to the Lake District, and, for the first time in his life, saw a forest. He looked at it, then looked at his teacher, then flashed all his fingers up and down.

The poetic response is not the only strategy people have for making meanings, but again I think the principle involved in this extract from a biology lesson is the same as that used by my young E.S.N.(S) friend. The teacher had done a demonstration in which carbon was burned in a test-tube and the gas given off bubbled through lime water, turning it milky. A student was given a piece of cheese to eat, and then she blew through a flask of lime water, again turning it milky.

> *Teacher:* You see that the carbon burnt up? Well, you do the
> same in your body. You burn up the cheese inside you.
> *Student 1:* Do I burn up my food inside me?
> *Student 2:* I had Weetabix this morning. Was that burnt up as
> well?
> *Student 3:* What did you have for breakfast?
> *Student 4:* Cornflakes. Was that burnt up too?
> *Teacher:* Yes.

The students were presented with a new and unfamiliar meaning of an old and familiar term – 'burnt up', and they responded by creating new contexts for the term so that they could test its appropriateness. The E.S.N.(S) boy looking at the forest was presented with an experience so unfamiliar that all the meaning options open to him were inappropriate, yet so insistent that it demanded a response. So he too extended the meaning of a familiar sign to accomodate the new experience.

We can now see how very far from reality the 'define-these-words' exercise is. Learning to make meanings is more than increasing your vocabulary; it is also learning how to exploit the overlapping, cross-referring language structures that are available to you so that you can meet the demands made by new situations. Very often the meanings needed can be constructed from the resources you already have, because the meaning choices encoded in language intersect and overlap with each other. In these cases, making a meaning consists not in adding an item to an inventory, but in extending and reordering items that are functioning and complete.

Contexts

Instead of using a 'definitions' approach to meaning, I want to explore the possibilities of a very different method in the classroom. This method is based on the (unpublished) work of Professor W. Haas, and it is consistent with the contextual approach I have been advocating.

Let us return to the biology students who were discussing the idea of something being 'burnt up'. If we paraphrase a little we can see that they are intuitively analysing and exploring contexts of the phrase 'burnt up':

The carbon was burnt up.

The cheese was burnt up.

The food was burnt up.

The Weetabix was burnt up.

The cornflakes was burnt up.

The method adopted intuitively by these students may be adopted consciously and systematically by teachers and learners. Let us begin with the relations, clearly illustrated here, between discovering unfamiliar meanings and exploring familiar meanings. We saw that the 'definitions' approach to meanings encourages teachers to place most of the emphasis on unfamiliar meanings. After all, what would be the point of a question like this in an English textbook?

Define these words: night, child, stand, fire.

Fortunately many students have profounder and more sensitive semantic intuitions than the writers of English textbooks. I shall use some of these intuitions as a concrete basis for explaining and exemplifying some of the linguistic strategies that may be adopted for exploring and discovering meanings.

The following text was written by one of my students, Denise, who had been asked to write an appeal, aimed at young children, to be careful with fireworks:

An Appeal to be carefull on Nov 5th

Bonfire Night the night that becomes a nightmare for some poor child who spends the night in a hospital. The night parents worry in case it's their child. So children make sure it's not you who spends the night in hospital and put your parents' minds at rest by being extra careful.

Don't stand to near a bonfire, the sparks that jump out every second could so easily set alight to your clothes.

And the wood that's burning could topple over hitting you.

Keep fire works a good distance away from the fire in a sealed box in case they catch alight and flare up in your hand.

Let somebody older light the firework's for you.

Don't throw fireworks they could hit somebody burning them severely

If you think a firework is not lit dont go up to it to find out it might be lit. If you go near it, it could flare up in your face.

Denise is playing with fire; not with real fire, but with the meanings of 'fire'. At one level we can describe her experiments with 'fire' just in terms of the words and phrases she uses – 'Bonfire, sparks, set alight, burning . . .' By going through the meaning options that are operating on this lexical level, we can arrive at a deeper level of semantic choice which Denise is exploiting as a basic element in the whole meaning of her appeal.

Before I show how these methods can apply to this student's work I would like to show how they work with some near-synonyms taken at random from Roget's Thesaurus. For example, 'soft(ly)' and 'tender(ly)' are fairly similar in meaning. This fact consists in (or at least is reflected in) the fact that they share very many contexts – in many sentences you could replace one by the other. So:

He touched her hair *softly*.

He touched her hair *tenderly*.

The bruised skin felt *soft*.

The bruised skin felt *tender*.

But there are also differences in meaning between the two words, and we can bring these differences out by finding contexts in which one may occur and the other may not:

The snow was *soft*.

*The snow was *tender*.

He stuck in the *soft* mud.

*He was stuck in the *tender* mud.

Similarly with 'plain' and 'simple'. There are contexts where either may be used without producing an odd sentence:

The answer was *plain*.

The answer was *simple*.

I like *plain* food.

I like *simple* food.

And there are contexts where only one could be used:

The fieldsman took a *simple* catch.

??The fieldsman took a *plain* catch.

I like *plain* chocolate.

??I like *simple* chocolate.

The fact that difference in meaning will always show up in difference of use in contexts provides the basis for a useful linguistic approach to the exploration of meaning in the classroom.

As I have suggested, a linguistic approach to meanings concerns itself, paradoxically, not with meanings themselves but with relations between meanings. For our purposes I shall take the central relation to be *difference of meaning*. For example it is obvious that there are differences of meaning between 'sparks' and 'wood'. The differences are so obvious that any method could capture them. But we are going to impose constraints on our methods to ensure that they conform to these conditions:

(a) The differences in meaning between two terms should be made clear from the way those terms function in contexts.
(b) The contexts should be taken, wherever possible, from texts written (or spoken) by students.
(c) The method should be capable of being broken down into simple steps.
(d) Each step should exploit linguistic resources already available to the students.

To fulfil the second condition, let us list the contexts, simplified a little, of 'sparks' and 'wood'.

The *sparks* that jump out . . .

The *sparks* . . . could . . . set alight to your clothes.

The *wood* that's burning . . .

The *wood* . . . could topple over hitting you.

Each of these four contexts can now be used as a test-bed in much the same way as we used paradigms in chapter 3. If 'sparks' and 'wood' are different in meaning, and if meaning does depend on context, then the differences should reveal themselves in the way the two terms relate to different contexts. If we put both terms in the first context, 'The —— that jump(s) out . . .' they both seem equally acceptable:

The *sparks* that jump out . . .

The *wood* that jumps out . . .

(We can ignore the difference between 'jump' and 'jumps', because it is pretty clearly a grammatical difference.)

The third context gives the same result:

The *sparks* that are burning . . .

The *wood* that is burning . . .

But in the second context, 'sparks' is more likely than 'wood', though 'wood' is possible:

The *sparks* could set alight to your clothes.

?The *wood* could set alight to your clothes.

In the fourth context 'sparks' is extremely unlikely, and 'wood' quite acceptable:

*The *sparks* could topple over hitting you.

The *wood* could topple over hitting you.

These tests, which are only a formalized and structured version of the methods used intuitively by the biology students quoted earlier, use only the very simple fact that the meaning of a word is very closely related to the way it is used.

If we wanted to take the method further we could go on and think of other contexts that would differentiate between 'sparks' and 'wood', but even then the method remains as simple – and as easy to handle in the classroom – as the one I have outlined. We can make the method even simpler by not insisting on total unacceptability of a word in a context to prove difference of meaning. Prof. W. Haas suggests that it is enough that one term is *more normal* than another in one context.

To take two previous examples – those of 'soft' and 'tender', and 'plain' and 'simple' – the fact that (b) and (d) (below) would be more normal than (a) and (c), even though all are perfectly legitimate English sentences, indicates that there are differences of meaning. And it may help us to work out what those differences arc:

(a) The steak was *soft*.

(b) The steak was *tender*.

(c) Chemistry is a *plain* subject.

(d) Chemistry is a *simple* subject.

And in differentiating 'sparks' and 'wood', it would have been enough just to prove that they were different in meaning to have shown that 'sparks' was more normal than 'wood' in

The —— could set alight to your clothes.

Other contexts not in the passage could also be used for the same purpose. Thus (f) is more normal than (e):

(e) The *wood* flew up the chimney.

(f) The *sparks* flew up the chimney.

If enough differentiating contexts were collected it would be possible to work out what the differences in meaning were between the two terms, and thus students could come to have the same advantages as lexicographers.

The differences in meaning between 'sparks' and 'wood' are intuitively obvious. The real test for this method comes when we try to make more subtle distinctions. The differences in meaning between 'burning' and 'alight', for example, are not at all obvious. The reader may care to experiment; try to say, just using definitions, what the differences in meaning are, then compare the adequacy of these definitions with the conclusions reached by using the contextual method. If we try to separate the meanings by definitions then, as far as the students are concerned, there is no test for the correctness of the definitions except the opinion of the teacher. Using the contextual method we can establish some interesting differences of use without going far beyond the contexts provided by the text.

With practice a class could set up the following functions which begin to show differences between the terms:

The wood that's *burning* . . .

The wood that's *alight* . . .

If you think a firework is not *burning* don't go up to it.

If you think a firework is not *alight* don't go up to it.

The exploration can be extended by using another technique introduced in chapter 3 – that of substitution. Some substitutions for 'wood' might give us more clues about the difference in meaning between 'burning' and 'alight'. For example:

(1) The light-bulb that's *alight* . . .
(2) The light-bulb that's *burning* . . .

(2) is more normal than (1).

(1) The dinner that's *alight* . . .
(2) The dinner that's *burning* . . .

(2) is more normal than (1).

(1) The sun that's *alight* . . .
(2) The sun that's *burning* . . .

(2) is more normal than (1).

The fact that light-bulbs and dinners can 'burn' but are not normally 'alight' might suggest that the range of meanings of 'burning' is wider than that of 'alight'. That the sun can 'burn', but is not normally said to be 'alight' might suggest that being alight may be a relatively temporary state, whereas burning may be relatively permanent.

By using these techniques it is possible to arrive at one of the main themes of the text. We may begin to see this if we work through some of the contexts that are provided in the text for 'light' (the verb) and 'set alight to' on the one hand, and 'burn' and 'flare up' on the other.

(3) The sparks could *light* your clothes.
(4) The sparks could *set alight to* your clothes.

(4) is more normal than (3).

(5) Let someone older *light* the fireworks for you.

(6) Let someone older *set alight to* the fireworks for you.

(5) is more normal than (6). In other usages and dialects 'set alight to' is ungrammatical, and 'set (something) alight' or set light to would be preferred. For Denise, 'set alight to' is a valid grammatical construction.

These contexts might suggest that 'lighting' is something done deliberately, whereas 'setting alight to' may either be deliberate or accidental, and that 'lighting' is normally done by people, whereas 'setting alight to' something may either be done by people or by such things as sparks. The reader might find it instructive to find other contexts which explore these issues in more detail. We can work out differences of meaning in a similar way if we turn to the difference between 'burn' and 'flare up', again substituting both in contexts taken from the passage:

(7) The wood that's *burning* . . .

(8) The wood that's *flaring up* . . .

(7) is more normal than (8), though both are perfectly good.

(9) A fireword (could) *burn* in your face.

(10) A firework (could) *flare up* in your face.

(10) is more normal than (9). In fact, it is difficult to think of a way in which (9) could be made to make sense.

We would need a lot more contexts to prove it, but following these tentative conclusions, we can suggest that one of the differences between 'burn' and 'flare up' is that 'flare up' suggests a more unstable type of combustion, one that might happen unexpectedly, hence its use with 'fireworks' rather than 'wood'. We could test this theory by seeing how well 'burn' and 'flare up' go with 'suddenly':

(11) It *flared up* suddenly.

(12) ?It *burned* suddenly.

(11) is more normal than (12).

This difference might become more evident if we expand (7) and (8) with the word 'gently'. This time we find that 'flare up' does not co-occur very happily with the extra word:

(13) The wood that's *burning* gently . . .

(14) ?The wood that's *flaring up* gently . . .

What we have learnt here we can now re-apply to 'light' and 'set alight to'. If we examine the possible co-occurrences of each we can begin to see the differences:

(15) I think I'll *light* the gas fire.
(16) I think I'll *set alight to* the gas fire.

(15) is more normal than (16).

(17) I think I'll *light* my cigarette.
(18) I think I'll *set alight to* my cigarette.

(17) is more normal than (18).

(19) ?Someone's *lit* the house.
(20) Someone's *set alight to* the house.

(20) is more normal than (19).

(21) ?Someone's *lit* the forest.
(22) Someone's *set alight to* the forest.

(22) is more normal than (21).

Some things – like gas fires, cigarettes and fireworks – are intended to burn. Other things – like houses, forests and clothes are not. The first set tends to go with the verb 'light', and the second with 'set alight to'.

It should by now be clear that one of Denise's main themes was the control of something that is extremely difficult to control. She expresses the theme succinctly in an effective pun – 'the night that becomes a nightmare'. But she also expresses it in her choice of meanings throughout the text, continually using verbs that are used for situations which are uncontrolled, and setting against them verbs which are used for situations where some control exists. The reader might care to contrast the different implications for control of these pairs of words and phrases, taken from Denise's essay:

night – nightmare

put . . . at rest – worry

too near – a good distance away

These are semantic subtleties. But does Denise not have a right to know that they are subtleties that she has at her command, subtleties that she understands because they are contained in the way she uses language? At the very least she has as much right to know this as a teacher has to tell her that she cannot define 'integrated' or 'subtle' or 'capricious'.

One of the great advantages of this method of exploration is that discussion of other meaning choices can emerge quite naturally.

Denise exploits a contrast between what we may term 'the language of control' and the 'language of lack of control'. Once we as teachers recognize this we make available for ourselves other language situations in which this contrast is used.

The contrast is used in writing instructions for operating a machine, in describing how to do an experiment in biology, in teaching a child how to eat without making a mess, in writing a recipe and in many other situations. They all exploit the meaning choices offered by language, and they all offer students the opportunity to enrich the meanings available to them, and perhaps enable them to discover areas where meanings that are available in language have not yet been exploited by them. We are certainly never going to find out how students can deal with these situations by the hit-or-miss methods we find in many English textbooks.

I would like to add, as a kind of appendix to this chapter, a brief summary of the contextual method described. In schematic form the method is as follows:

(1) Choose the items whose meanings are to be examined.

(2) Write down the sentences or clauses in which they occur, simplifying them if necessary.

(3) (a) Write the first sentence again, substituting the second item for the first.

(b) Write the second sentence again, substituting the first item for the second.

(4) (a) Compare the relative normality of the first two sentences. If there is a difference of normality does it give any clues about the differences in meaning between the two items?

(b) Compare the relative normality of the second two sentences. If there is a difference of normality does this suggest anything about the differences in meaning between the two items?

(5) (a) Find other contexts in which one of the items can more normally occur than the other.

(b) Do these indicate anything about the differences in meaning?

5 Frameworks for language function

Language functions and social rules

Every sentence in every language is multi-functional. Thus the English sentence, 'John isn't very happy' could be used to assert an opinion, to suggest a course of action (implying, 'So why don't you go and talk to him?') or to start off a conversation. But before we can start looking at functions of language we must be clear what it is in language that can have a function. If we want to say, as we shall, 'The function of this is . . .' then we cannot be talking about sentences or words. Suppose the function we had in mind were that of referring to something, and that we had in mind the word 'John'. So 'The function of the word "John" is to refer to John'. If in a cross-word someone writes the word 'John' then that is just an occurrence of the word in the abstract. But if someone says, 'John's the one with black hair and glasses' in the course of a conversation then 'John' does refer to somebody. The difference is in the *use*. The word itself does not refer to anything, any more than the nonsense word 'binks' refers to anything. But somebody could use the word 'binks' to refer to somebody, perhaps as a nickname or a trade name. Words themselves do not have functions; to have a function a word must be used. The same goes for sentences; 'John is daft' as I have just written it – as an example of an English sentence illustrating the structure 'subject + "is" + subject complement' – does not say anything about anybody. But it could be used to say that John is daft if somebody wanted to say that.

This is an important preliminary distinction because it means that we must approach the problem by looking at particular uses of language in their whole context, not at artificial, abstract examples of language. In chapter 4 we saw the importance of the linguistic context for the study of meanings. In this chapter I must stress the importance of the whole context, the cultural, historical, political, social context. To show something of how these contexts relate to language I will take as an example this extract from a discussion with one of my classes about the occurrence of the sentence 'Burslem Booters Rule OK'.

> *J.K.:* What about this? You've all seen things like this: 'Burslem Booters Rule OK'.
> *Steve:* . . . Written on toilet walls.
> *Tony:* Walls in the street. Street walls.
> *J.K.:* Yeah. Anywhere where there's space.
> *Tony:* They do it with aerosol sprays.
> *Steve:* . . . More distinctive.
> *J.K.:* What does it mean?
> *Steve:* It's – a psychological outlet, isn't it?
> *J.K.:* Perhaps it is. But that's not what it *means*. Simon?
> *Simon:* It's local kids, you know.
> *J.K.:* Uh hm. That's – those are the people who are doing the writing. But – em – Burslem Booters are not, so far as we know, in charge of the government. So what does 'Rule' mean?
> *Erica:* No-one dares disagree with them. They rule.
> *Robert:* They'd get booted in.
> *J.K.:* What is it people daren't disagree with?
> *Steve:* They probably rule Burslem. They're the town skinheads. They go round terrorizing people and that. Having trouble with the police. There's no rival group of people in that town that can harm them.
> *J.K.:* Could a rival group harm them? Are they really that tough?
> *John:* Only because there's a lot of them all together.
> *J.K.:* Where else might you see this sort of thing?

> *Tony:* If you go out of town like. If you go to London on some
> walls you can see 'Man United Rule OK'. Something like
> that.
>
> *Steve:* Or Macc, like. We went on holiday to North Wales. We
> went to this place – this pub. It says, 'Macc Skins Rule'.
> You know. (laughter)
>
> *J.K.:* Sort of – a bit like invading somebody else's territory.
>
> *Paul:* Like dogs do when they do it against a lamp post every so
> often. When other dogs smell it – y' know, this is such-a-
> dog's territory. Don't trespass.
>
> *J.K.:* Yeah. In spite of the element of vulgarity, that's a fair
> example. There's plenty of other animals give a territorial
> sign.
>
> *Robert:* Robins – don't they – er – sing?
>
> *J.K.:* Yeah. It sounds pretty till you know what it means. What
> about us humans? What territorial signs have we got?
> Erica?
>
> *Erica:* 'Keep Out' signs.
>
> *Steve:* Trespassers will be persecuted. (laughter) Or when there's
> 'private' on the door.

The examples were multiplied, and their particular functions were
discussed in the course of the lesson. Because we need a corpus to
begin our examination of the language functions involved in
'Burslem Booters Rule OK' and related utterances I shall present
some examples. Some are taken from this class's discussion and one
or two are my own. There are many ways of marking an area of space
for prohibition of entry. They include 'Keep Out', 'Private',
'Trespassers will be prosecuted', 'Staff Only', 'Gentlemen' (on
toilets), 'No Parking'. There are also many ways of marking a space
as allowing entry: 'Welcome' (said to a visitor), 'Do come in', 'No
obligation to buy' (in a shop window), 'Gentlemen' (on toilets).
Notice that 'Gentlemen' figures in both categories because its context
defines a two-group set, one group of which is thereby implicitly
prohibited, and the other group explicitly allowed, entry. It illus-
trates the point that *words* do not have functions, only particular
words in particular contexts. As well as marking places in this way we
can also mark other things, which I will call, for want of a better
term, 'situations'. The 'Confidential' on a letter or report is functionally close enough to 'Private' on a door to be included in the same

class, but clearly does not mark exclusion from a *place*. Similarly 'RU 18' in the form of a number plate often displayed in pubs is not so much a prohibition to enter at all as a prohibition to take part in the drinking. The same might go for 'X certificate' on a film poster, and 'Top Secret' on a document. Obviously 'RU 18' and 'Cert. X' shade into the 'place' category, but there is some justification for keeping them separate. To keep things symmetrical; there are ways of marking an activity as allowing entry: 'Dip. Ed.' marks the legitimacy of a teacher's activities in formal education. 'Oh, yes there is' said by the principal boy at a pantomime marks the legitimacy of the response, 'Oh, no there isn't'. 'Do you come here often?' (or whatever young men say to young ladies at dances these days) marks an invitation to participate in the activity of being chatted up. My name and address on an envelope marks my right to read the contents.

What we have done so far consists of taking two steps which are standard procedures in a linguistic investigation. We have constructed a corpus of utterance-uses. And we have assigned each member of the corpus to a class. In fact our method was more complicated; we started with one utterance-use, 'Burslem Booters Rule OK', assigned a class name – 'Territorial' – to it; found other members of the same class – 'Keep Out' . . .; set up another class within the larger 'Territorial' class of utterance-uses allowing entry; found utterance-uses which were members of that class; then set up another two classes with members whose functions paralleled the first two, and found utterance-uses to fit them. The steps seem complicated put like this, but in fact the whole process amounts to the two very simple steps of setting up a corpus and classifying its members. So we have in schematic form:

	ALLOW	PROHIBIT
PLACE	'Do come in' . . .	'Private' . . .
SITUATION	'Do you come here often' . . .	'Top Secret' . . .

The advantages of setting things out in a simple structure become clear once we see that we can do more than just allow and prohibit access to property; we can encourage it, tolerate it, allow it on certain conditions and so on. And all these things apply to more than just one kind of place and situation; an office and a forest are very different places, but they may both be treated as 'out of bounds'. Reading a letter is not the same as drinking in a pub, but both may be marked as prohibited. The simple structure allows us to see our way through all these complicating factors and to treat the problem in a more systematic way.

Another advantage of a simple structure like this is that it may be used as a framework for classroom activity. In any social organization, whether it be home, school, a hospital, a town or a whole society, there are rules which determine under what circumstances people may do things and go places. Part of the process of education is learning how those rules work in practice, and most of this 'informal' education takes place outside the formal curriculum, and the rationale for these rules and constraints is rarely made explicit. Our society is an exceedingly complex one, and it is important that young people in the process of learning the rules should have opportunities to exchange and organize the information that they already have. In fact many of the discussions in students' common rooms, playgrounds, homes, coffee bars, pubs consist of talk which explores the boundaries of the group; what you can and cannot do at home or at school, where you are not allowed to go, with whom and why. Bringing these issues into the classroom is no more than an acknowledgement that the issues are real and pressing to the students.

There are many ways of doing this, and each teacher will find approaches best suited to the particular class. I shall simply give some examples of how I have approached these topics with classes. My own focus with topics like this is always on the forms of communication that are used to transmit the rules. After all, even unwritten rules are not transmitted by magic, and language is the chief means used to express the relevant instructions, advice, warnings.

After the initial discussion I gave each student in the class a copy of the official college rules, and asked them to discuss and write down where you are and are not allowed to go in college and under what circumstances, and what you are and are not allowed to do. Then we discussed the reasons why each of these rules existed, and I asked the students, working in groups, to write down as many of the 'unwritten' college rules as possible, and we explored differences between the written, official rules and the unwritten, unofficial rules. We did the same kind of analysis of the students' homes, and of other situations like trains, football matches, pubs. Then I asked the students to find out from friends and relatives what the unwritten rules were at their places of work, and we discussed that.

I do not claim that this is particularly original; it does not, I think, constitute a revolutionary new educational method. What I would claim is important about it is that it began from a discussion of a peer-group utterance, and in many ways the language of one's peer group is the language of central importance to oneself. And this way of going about things demands from the teacher that he be prepared to hold the peer-group language of his students as worthy of serious study. Our analysis has borne some fruit so far, but I think it is possible to push it still further.

How do these messages relate to the cultural, historical, political, social contexts that I mentioned earlier? And can these things be explored in the classroom? One approach to the first question might be to consider what socio-cultural assumptions are necessary for these messages to be meaningful at all. Take 'Cert. X' for example. This would make no sense if there were no censoring body to impose the category. And this body must, over time, act in response to the attitudes and values of those groups in society which can exert influence over it. Some of these groups may have attitudes which derive from religious or historical attitudes or from aesthetic or cultural convictions. And 'Cert. X' can only be meaningful if there are legal and moral pressures which enforce the rules for which it stands. Obviously the pyramid of which 'Cert. X' is the tip can be as deep as you care to make it.

In the same way, the meaningfulness of 'Top Secret' depends on the existence of political attitudes and institutions, on attitudes towards science, on the existence and form of political alliances and conflicts. And the meaningfulness of 'Do you come here often?' depends on a network of rules and conventions which determine how we may and may not get to know people in our society. These – and many other – simple utterances are deeply embedded in our society.

Methods of analysis

When someone is learning a language he learns it as a means for achieving certain ends. He does not, for example, learn grammatical rules in a vacuum, but as a means of fulfilling certain functions that happen to be important to him. He finds himself in widely differing situations, and he learns that different forms of language are appropriate in them. He develops what Dell Hymes (1972) calls *communicative competence*. That is, he learns when and when not to speak, how formally to speak, what tones are appropriate and inappropriate, what can be said and what cannot. Every speaker also develops a model of what functions language can serve, and he uses that model to filter out unacceptable responses. But just as every speaker can use the grammatical rules of his language without necessarily being able to state them explicitly, so every speaker 'knows' the functional resources his language makes available to him without necessarily being able to make them explicit. Teachers, however, do need a fairly accurate, explicit model of language functions. Without it, the tasks they set students will tend to be biased in favour of the functions they intuitively feel to be important, to the detriment of other, equally important, functions.

Several interesting theories of language function have been published recently. The reader may care to refer particularly to M. A. K. Halliday's *Explorations in the Functions of Language* (1973) and to J. Britton's *The Development of Writing Abilities (11–18)* (1975), details of which are included in 'Further Reading'. But teachers need more than a theory; they need *methods* for working out what models of language function are presented in their students' speech and writing. Such methods are important because the model of language function a teacher brings to the classroom is likely to be different to that of his students. The model which dominates education is what Halliday calls the *representational* model. This states that the main function of language is to communicate information. This information may be objective, as in 'Shakespeare wrote *Hamlet*', or subjective, as in 'I'm feeling sad'. It is this function which is exploited when a teacher lectures and a class takes notes, and it is this function which a student must fulfil in writing up a science experiment, or writing an essay in history or geography. It is this function which people have in mind when they require 'clear, simple English', perhaps because this is the function that has the most tangible economic value.

How 'basic' in fact is this function? Let us try to answer this by asking what functions of language human beings could not do without. To answer this question we may look at the early language stages of a child. For him the basic functions are those which impinge upon his direct needs. For him the statement, 'I'm hungry' is not an attempt to convey information about his inner state to someone – it is a means of getting someone to do something. The language we would need to get by on would consist of requests and complaints, not of statements of fact about the world. However the representational function is a valid and, in our society, a necessary one, and it must take its place on the curriculum. But it is important for teachers to remember that this function develops out of others, and that students must be given time and opportunity to assimilate their skills in other functions as a basis for learning how to exploit information-conveying functions.

Let us look at an example of a gap between a teacher's and a student's model of language function. In the course of a series of lessons on different types of 'official' language I asked a class to write instructions about what to do when you go to vote. Here is one set of instructions:

Going to Vote

It is quite simple. All you do is take your voteing card to the poling station. This card tells you which poling station to vote at and gives you your number. This card will be coming to you by post any day now. If you forget the card do not worrie, tell them at the desk your name and address and you have forgotten your card. The poling station are open from 7 a.m. to 10 p.m. in which time you can go and vote.

In setting the exercise, my intention was to focus on how information and instructions should be ordered to achieve maximum clarity. The concern of this writer was somewhat different as we can see if we analyse the passage functionally. The methods I shall use are basically the same as I used in discussing 'Burslem Booters Rule OK'. They consist simply of classifying utterances together using fairly intuitive criteria, then generalizing from the classifications. Take the first sentence: 'It is quite simple'. Intuitively, this seems to have the same function as the phrase 'All you do . . .' and a similar function to '. . . do not worrie'. None of these are intended to convey information or to tell the reader what to do. Their function in the passage is to reassure the reader. The actual instructions given to the reader consist of 'take your voteing card . . .' and 'tell them at the desk . . .' The rest of the passage consists of background information.

Generalizing the three functions as reassurance, instruction and information, the passage can be neatly analysed:

Reassurance	It is quite simple.
	All you do . . .
	. . . do not worrie
Instruction	Take your voteing card . . .
	Tell them at the desk . . .
Information	This card . . . your number.
	This card . . . any day now.
	The poling station . . . go and vote.

This may be quite interesting from a theoretical point of view, though it may seem not to have any direct practical application. But it does have. The great advantage of using linguistic methods, as I have shown in previous chapters, is that they enable teachers to work from students' strengths to their weaknesses. Here the student has recognized that many people fear the process of voting, particularly if they have never voted before, or if they have mislaid their voting card. He has therefore built into his instructions some explicit reassurance to help allay these fears.

His weakness is not having enough detailed instructions or information. He does not say how to find out where your polling station is if you have lost your card, and he does not prepare the uninitiated voter for what happens after he has handed in his voting card. The question now is, how can we get from this student's strength to his weakness? The link is fairly obvious: what we want is that the student should reassure his readers about the simplicity of voting, not just by saying it is simple, but by giving the reader enough information to pre-empt any fears and doubts there might be. Thus we may discuss with the student why it was necessary to say 'It is quite simple' and so on, and how he can achieve ends in other ways. We might get some of the class to act out the process as faithfully as possible, to find out where doubts and confusions occur. A teacher may be able to see this kind of point intuitively, but it is much easier to see and to work with if the teacher has a relatively objective, explicit method to start from.

From the student's point of view the process I have just described assimilates one language function to another. He is being asked to reduce the number of explicit functions used in his passage by one, and to realize that function through another. 'Reassurance' is a separable, discrete function in the passage I have quoted; in a rewritten version it would not be separable but would be part of a more general organization. This process – Halliday terms it 'functional reduction' – is an important part of language development because it increases the number of ways there are of using language to achieve intentions.

It may be instructive to analyse the work of a student who has achieved a degree of functional reduction in her work. The question, 'Explain in 250 words the functions and working of an electric drill', is of a kind familiar to teachers working with English Language examination syllabuses. It gives no clues as to what sort of reader the writing is intended for. It normally prohibits the use of diagrams – an essential part of real instructions. Consequently the writer is forced to work in a linguistic vacuum. Her answer is as follows:

> (1)An electric drill usually has a long thin point on the end, which is the standered attachment on the modern, up-to-date drill. (2)If when using an electric drill one is not careful one could find a large hole in the palm of one's hand. (3) Electric drills have many functions and attatchments. (4)One function the drill has with the attachment that looks like a circular saw, is to saw through corrugated plastics (5)and would probably annihilate one's main artery in the wrist and leave one's body stone dead, (6)(very nice, (7)always good to lend to the neighbour one particularly hates when he has had one too many at the local) – (8)nasty business. (9)Another function the electric drill has is a sandpapering block (10)which quivers at an obnoxious speed (11)and do fatal damage to one's body if applied on a soft part of the flesh e.g. the buttocks or under the armpits. (12)This could make one experience excruciating agony. (13)So a good tip is to keep it locked away from the wife (14)as if she gets in a bad mood and the drill complete with sandpaper could be responsible for the absence of skin on the upper part of one's legs.

> (I shall refer to the passage by the bracketed numbers, which should be taken as referring to the sentence, clause or phrase following.)

This analysis is fairly informal, and the reader is free to analyse it differently. The passage contains only four sentences of the sort we would normally expect in an exercise like this. They are (1), (3), (4) and (9), and they have a fairly clear informative function. I will include (10) in this group, even though 'obnoxious' indicates personal feelings. (2) seems to have two related functions; to shock and to give a kind of safety warning. The same function is fulfilled by (5), (11) and, less obviously, by (12) which again suggests the writer's personal feelings about these gruesome possibilities. The most unequivocal personal comments are (6) and (8). (7) and (14) both explore what *might* happen if this object were to be used by others, and the use of language to express possibilities and hypothetical situations involves an imaginative function. Although much of the passage is tacitly concerned with what to do and what not to do with an electric drill, the only explicit statement on these lines is (13), which attempts to fulfil a regulative function. We may set out these groupings systematically:

Informative	*Warning/shock*	*Personal*	*Regulative*	*Imaginative*
(1)	(2)			
(3)				
(4)	(5)	(6)		(7)
		(8)		
(9)				
(10)	(11)			
	(12)		(13)	(14)

As an answer to the question set, bearing in mind the conventions that govern this kind of exercise, this will not do. The writer has said little about the primary functions of an electric drill, and nothing about its working. The writer has chosen instead to write in a different mode to that required. Unlike the writer of 'Going to Vote' she uses the informative function of language as a starting-point for what J. Britton *et al.* (1975) call *poetic* writing. This is writing in which 'The writer is concerned to create relations internal to the work, and achieve a unity, a construct discrete from actuality'. This internal unity is what the writer has created, using a repetition of movement from the informative to the imaginative, and relating her writing not to practical needs, but to personal and emotional considerations. In this kind of writing you can make your own rules for reading; if you are not sure about the purposes and conventions of the piece you are intended to write, then creating your own rules is an obvious option.

And judged by its own rules this piece is not unsuccessful. In fact the way the writer constantly returns to the intended function shows that she does have a grasp of it, but chooses to subordinate it to others.

If she is to develop her ability to write impersonally then she needs contexts in which such writing makes sense. After all language only has a variety of functions because speakers have a variety of needs, and these needs must be in the forefront of a writer's mind when he is constructing a text.

From the analyses of these two passages we can generalize a little further. The categories I isolated were:

Passage 1. Reassurance; instruction; informative.

Passage 2. Informative; warning/shock; personal; regulative; imaginative.

The 'informative' category figures in both passages. 'Instruction' and 'regulation' are both to do with getting the reader to act in specified ways, so they may be grouped together as a single category. 'Reassurance' and 'warning/shock' are similar in that they are attempting to induce in the reader an attitude towards his actions. So the functions we now have are:

Informative

Regulative (including instruction and various types of regulation of behaviour)

Affective (including reassurance and warning/shock)

Personal

Imaginative

Analysis of other passages would give us many more categories, and many more examples of the categories we already have. I shall not proliferate categories here because I am more concerned with methods for arriving at an analysis and with relations between categories. However, readers may care to take the exercise further and work out a more exhaustive set of functions used in their students' writing and speech. Conclusions will differ from person to person, but this is not very important; what is important is how the categories get related to each other, and what use they are put to in the classroom. For example, other teachers may disagree with me about grouping together language which is intended to reassure and language which is intended to warn. They may prefer to say that reassurance establishes a special relationship with the reader, and that since the end result of a warning is that the reader should do (or not do) something, warning has a regulative function, and reassurance, perhaps, an interactional one. What matters to us is whether these functions, however they are conceived, receive opportunities for use in the classroom; whether they are able to reflect the way language is used in the course of students' everyday lives.

Relations between categories

As I have already mentioned, it is part of a speaker's natural language development that functions become fulfilled by more and more abstract and indirect means. The need for this skill in human society is dictated by the complexity of social relations and the need to maintain and reinforce them. To take a simple example, if you want to get John to shut the door, and John is a personal friend, you can simply tell him, 'Shut the door, John.' But if John is a distant acquaintance, you might prefer to say, 'It's rather cold in here with the door open.' You cannot use a regulative function directly in these circumstances, but you can use an informative function which makes real a regulative function. A similar point about the social constraints on the use of language functions is made by a joke about a blunt R.S.M. who has to inform one of his soldiers about a recent bereavement. Instead of using an informative function directly, he realizes the informative function through that function which most appropriately expresses his relation to the soldier – the regulative function: 'All men with fathers still alive take one pace forward. Private Smith, stay where you are.'

The ability to use a language function not just to achieve an end, but as a means for realizing a different function is obviously something that is acquired slowly and with difficulty. It is important enough to warrant more examples so that the complexity of what must be learned is appreciated. If we just take the five categories we generated earlier, then we have no less than twenty ways of realizing the functions. Some examples are as follows: informative statements can be used to produce, say, a reassuring effect, or a reassuring statement can be used to provide a piece of information. A doctor who has successfully operated on a dangerously ill patient may say to the patient's wife, 'The operation was successful' thereby reassuring her, but doing it *through* a piece of information. (Affective *realized through* informative.) Or he may say, 'You've nothing to worry about now.' thereby informing her of the operation's success, but doing so *through* the medium of reassurance. (Informative *realized through* affective.) Other possibilities are:

Regulative realized through personal:
  I don't like you doing that.
Personal realized through regulative:
  Don't bring that spider anywhere near me!
Imaginative realized through regulative:
  You don't see me creeping up behind you. (Said in the context of a children's game.)

Teachers can do little to control the precise means a student uses to achieve his aims in writing. What teachers can control is the simulated social situation which provides the context for students' writings, and which determines the approximate approaches for solving the problem involved. For example, presenting students with a situation which calls for the use of tact gives them an opportunity to practice the kind of indirect language skills I have been discussing. The skills are often required in conversations which need some social distance to be maintained, and in many kinds of formal speech and writing. Some of these situations will already be very familiar to students; others they may not experience until later in their lives. In this area of language study it is relatively easy to find skills which can be used as a basis for developing and extending abilities. For example, most sixteen-year-olds, of both sexes, are familiar with the utterance 'I'm sorry, I'm washing my hair that night'. I have used this utterance as the starting-point for a study of language which ended in an exploration of the language of Parliament and the law courts. I was able to do this because in each case special conventions govern the language functions that can be used. If we take the most famous example of 'un-Parliamentary' parliamentary language, Churchill's accusation of a Member perpetrating a 'terminological inexactitude', we can see that this has much in common with the quoted excuse for not going out with someone:

(1) In both situations the use of language to achieve a direct insult or rejection is proscribed.
(2) In both situations the *effect* of insult or rejection is achieved indirectly, through purporting to use a language function other than the intended one.

(3) In both situations the utterance has become so convention-alized that the indirectness has become almost transparent. Since both parties normally understand its implications, 'I'm washing my hair' is almost equivalent to saying, 'I don't fancy you.' To people who know the story, 'terminological in-exactitude' simply means 'lie' and has no ambiguity about it at all.

Between the very familiar experiences of making excuses, dropping hints, being tactful, and the very remote contexts like Parliament and the courts there is a whole spectrum of situations, all of which may usefully be used to help students master the multitudinous language functions that are so essential in our complex, changing society.

Development of language functions

To conclude, I would like to demonstrate that it is possible for students, starting with one model for the application of language functions, to develop a more adequate application through an increased awareness of social constraints. I asked a class of part-time business studies students to prepare a report based on complaints about staff behaviour in their offices. The reports were to be written for posting up on the notice board for all the staff to read.

Staff Behaviour. Week starting 8/8/75 ending 15/8/75

There has been a lot of complaints about staff behaviour recently. A lot of people have been coming in very late, and they have not been reporting this to the management. Reasons for lateness must allways be given to Mr Leech from now on, or the person con-cerned will be dismissed.

Also the canteen is often in a bad mess. Staff are leaving litter about, and spilling Tea, Coffee etc. without clearing up. Any mess in the canteen must be cleared up by 1.30. And you must not smoke in the canteen.

Staff have the same bad attitude to equipment, with pens and pecils biten, and typewriters being badly used, and ribben stored carelessly.

All these things must be put right at once.

Discussion of the passages written by the class centred on the ques-tion of how the staff would react to the reports, and whether they would have any effect on behaviour. In discussing the report I have quoted, the class, most of whom do work in offices, agreed that it would put people's backs up, and perhaps make them behave even worse. I continued the discussion by getting the class to role-play staff and management in a meeting to discuss the reports, using this one as an example because it was the most critical. The pressures against the use of this very direct criticism became clear as the discussion turned into a confrontation, with 'staff' objecting to the tone of the criticism, and to the vague, unsubstantiated nature of the complaints, and 'management' trying to justify the report, as well as conceding that it might have been presented more tactfully. After the discussion, I asked the class to rewrite their reports using what they had learned from the discussion to make them as effective as possible. This student produced this rewritten version:

Staff Behaviour. Week starting 8/8/75 ending 15/8/75

LATE
during these two dates   6 people ten minetes late
                         2 people 30 minutes late
                         1 person 2 hours late
No reason was given for these late arrivels.

CANTEEN
                         Paper bags left on tables and floors
                         Tea, Coffee etc. spilt on tables and floor.
                         Food found behind water pipes.
                         People smoking though there is a no smoking sign.

EQUIPMENT
                         Pencils and pens were found to be biten.
                         Typewriters had been scratched because of banging.
                         Rubers had been defaced.
                         Typing riben was found to be stored in large boxes allowing them to unroll.

The functions represented in the first version are, roughly:

Informative: e.g. A lot of people have been coming in very late.

Regulative: e.g. And you must not smoke in the canteen.

Warning/threat: e.g. ... or the person concerned will be dismissed.

Personal: e.g. ... a bad mess; ... the same bad attitude.

By contrast the second version uses only one function – the informative. But all the functions used in the first passage, except the threat of dismissal, are present in the second passage. They are realized through the function which is accepted as the least controversial in this social situation. Other situations will require functions to be realized in other ways, and for the teacher this means finding out what situations students are likely to find themselves in, and how they do in fact cope with the language demands.

In this chapter I have dealt only with a small set of language functions, and only in the context of students' writing. I could have said much more about the different functions of talking in classrooms, and I could have included more detail on other functions of language. But this chapter has not tried to present a theory of language function, or a full-scale sociological analysis of language in education. It has been only about *methods* – about ways of analysing students' language to obtain a clearer idea of how a particular text works, and what directions are indicated for the next steps in the writer's language development.

6 Cohesion

Development

The following two pieces of writing were both written by the same sixteen-year-old student. I want to explore some questions about them.

(1) What language resources are exploited by the writer in order to achieve unity in these passages?

(2) What reasons might there be for the relative degrees of success in achieving unity?

(3) How might a better understanding of these resources be useful to a teacher?

Passage (a) *A New Savings Scheme*

Listen everybody! There is a new post office saving's scheme which has just come out, giving you much better service. You will have a higher interest on than before this savings scheme came into force. You will get $7\frac{1}{2}$ per cent. Much higher than before. If you are in long enough you will be able to take out a special savings, so that you can have a pension in your later years. You will also be able to get savings stamps. So come and join us for a better service. For every year that you save with us depending on how much you have got in we will give you some more money.

10 You won't have a better chance of saving. We are trying to give
you the best that we can. For your children, for every pound that
they put in we will give them a savings stamp worth twenty pence.
This is a scheme that you cannot miss. It gives you everything you
want.

Passage (b) *Accidents in Cheshire During the Day*

There are more accidents from noon to midnight than their are in
the morning. That I presume is the business time when there are
vehicles on the road.

There are quite a number of accidents which occur between 11
5 and 12pm. This is because of the people coming out of the pubs
and straight into their cars.

The most people that were in accidents were in the area of
Warrington in the month of August. Their were 57 accidents.

The most fatal accidents came from Chester. This is because of all
10 the tourists passing through.

Passage (a) was written in the context of an exploration of different
kinds of 'official' writing. Passage (b) was written in the course of an
exercise in writing about graphs and simple statistics. This passage
was about graphical representations of road accidents.

Passage (a) seems to me to read better. There is a liveliness that is
missing in passage (b). (a) seems more unified, whereas (b) reads like
a catalogue of facts. The functions, of course, are different. Passage
(b) fulfils only an informative function, and there seems to be no
clear sense of what reader is being written for. Passage (a), by contrast, fulfils several functions. It is informative, but it is also
regulatory – '. . . come and join us . . .', 'This is a scheme that you
cannot miss'. The frequent repetition of 'you' and 'us' and the appeal
to social values – 'We are trying to give you the best that we can' –
suggest a strong interactional function – an attempt to set up a
relationship with the reader.

These differences in the variety of functions being fulfilled come
out in several ways. One corresponding difference is in the variety of
grammatical structures used in each passage. The structures of passage (b) are quite limited in range, there being only four basic structures used:

(i) There + be + (noun phrase) + (place adverbial) + (time
adverbial)

    (ii) This + be + because of . . .
   (iii) This/that + be + time adverbial
   (iv) Noun phrase + be/came + place adverbial

The difference in range may be clear if we compare passage (a)'s structures:

     (i) You will have/get + noun phrase
    (ii) (So) Imperative
   (iii) (Four noun phrase), for (every) noun phrase we will give
       noun phrase
   (iv) There + be + noun phrase + (noun phrase as verb) +
       (verb-ing noun phrase)
    (v) This + be + noun phrase
   (vi) Pronoun + verb to you + noun phrase
  (viii) If . . . you will . . . so that . . .

    (Items in brackets are *optional*. That is, they are only used in some
    of the structures covered.)

It must be stressed that these are not formal or rigorous presentations of the grammatical structures. They are simply an impressionistic summing-up of differences between the two passages' exploitations of grammatical resources. I must also stress the dangers of drawing conclusions about the writer's language competence from these passages. The way each passage is dealt with tells us much more about the relationship between the writer's language resources and the tasks set than it does about those resources *per se*. So, for example, the writer, for passage (b), was given a set of facts about accidents in Cheshire and asked to explain them. The structure that must inevitably suggest itself is 'Statement of fact + proposed explanation'. Readers are invited to ask themselves how many times it would be possible to repeat that pattern without repeating grammatical structures. In fact, given the restrictions imposed by the task the writer varies the structures quite well, mixing 'There + be . . .' with 'Noun phrase + verb . . .' By contrast, passage (a) has not only to fulfil a purely informative function, but uses the opportunity afforded by the interactional and regulatory functions to employ a variety of structures.

    The task involved in passage (a) allows for much greater scope to draw on grammatical structures. It is the task itself, and not the writer's language abilities, which explains the differences in quality between the two passages.

Another difference between the passages, as I noted earlier, is in the way they 'hang together'. Passage (a) reads to me as a unity, and passage (b) as disjointed. This unity is not just a matter of 'relevance'. Passage (b) as much as passage (a) sticks to its subject unwaveringly, and each constitutes a 'text'.

Halliday and Hasan (1976), on whose work my analyses depend heavily, define a text as 'any passage, spoken or written, of whatever length, that does form a unified whole'. And they enumerate some examples:

> A text may be . . . prose or verse, dialogue or monologue. It may be anything from a single proverb to a whole play, from a momentary cry for help to an all-day discussion on a committee.

This characterization is readily understood only because we already have some intuitive idea of what a text is. We can recognize, say, a piece of writing as a text more or less unreflectingly because we suppose a text to be unified by a particular expressive function. But the impression of unity that results from our acknowledgement of this function comes from our ability to interpret linguistic relations within the text. These relations are themselves the result of operations that the writer or speaker has performed on his text by exploiting the choices in language. I want to stress that the relations, operations and choices are linguistic and not literary. Literary interpretation depends for its meaningfulness on linguistic interpretation. I think it is important for teachers to be aware of this because many teachers take literary criteria to be primary when they are assessing a piece of writing.

To give a brief example, Ezra Pound's 'In a station of the metro' works by assuming intuitive linguistic interpretation:

In a station of the metro

The apparition of these faces in the crowd;
petals on a wet, black bough.

In making linguistic sense of this utterance we must assume that it constitutes a text. It is, for example, presented contiguously, and not with one line on page 2 and another line on page 30. The punctuation marks it as a single sentence. 'The' and 'these' presuppose some reference outside the sentence itself. The writer uses these clues to indicate that the passage is to be read as a single, unified text, and it is only on the basis of this assumption that we can begin to analyse it as a *literary* text.

One value of linguistics lies in its ability to make explicit the language resources that are being used in a particular text. Of course the English teacher is not only concerned with the abstract system of language, but also with particular instances of language use. Linguistics can provide contexts within which these particular instances may be understood and evaluated. I want to suggest some lines on which such a context may be constructed.

We are aware that passage (a) hangs together. We are aware that it is about one subject, and that it has a particular style. What we may not be explicitly aware of, though we experience it every time we try to write or say something, is that this 'hanging together' depends on how the writer resolves a number of tensions that constrain what he can say and how he says it. I shall only deal with one of these tensions: the tension between the need to develop the line of a text and the need for a text to constitute a single, finished unity.

The first section of (a) introduces its 'new' information by latching it on to information that the reader is presumed to have already: that is, that the post office already runs savings schemes. It is for this reason that 'a *new* post office saving's scheme *which has just come out*' is not tautologous. 'New' here refers to the innovatory nature of the scheme compared to earlier schemes. 'just come out' refers to the proximity to the present of the scheme's introduction.

Elliptical comparatives contribute to the relation between the information given and the presuppositions made: 'much better service', 'a higher interest on than before', 'much higher than before'. These comparatives all suggest comparison *with* something, and the obvious vehicle for comparison is the earlier savings schemes, which are not explicitly mentioned but which must be 'understood' by the reader. This framework allows the writer to establish the new information contained in the phrase, 'a new post office saving's scheme'. This new information then becomes 'given' information for the purposes of the rest of the passage, and the actual details of the scheme then become the *new* 'new information'. Thus, 'If you are in long enough . . .' presupposes that the reader understands that what he is 'in' is the new savings scheme. The elliptical nature of 'in long enough' both provides a context for the introduction of a piece of new information – 'you will be able to take out a special savings' –

and, as we shall see, contributes to the linguistic unity of the passage. These details about the new scheme then become used as given information for the purpose of making general comments on the scheme: 'You won't have a better chance of saving', 'This is a scheme that you cannot miss.' The process whereby new information becomes given provides the basis for development of most texts. We may represent this recursive, dialectical process schematically:

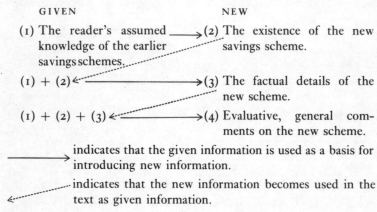

GIVEN   NEW

(1) The reader's assumed ⟶ (2) The existence of the new
    knowledge of the earlier   savings scheme.
    savings schemes.

(1) + (2) ⟵ ⟶ (3) The factual details of the
                                     new scheme.

(1) + (2) + (3) ⟵ ⟶ (4) Evaluative, general comments on the new scheme.

⟶ indicates that the given information is used as a basis for introducing new information.

⟵ indicates that the new information becomes used in the text as given information.

We may compare the relative developmental complexity of this text with that of passage (b). This passage, like the other, introduces its 'new' information by means of already-assumed information. This 'given' information coincides with the basic form of the first sentence – 'There are . . . accidents (in Cheshire).' The new information is to do with *when* there are accidents. In English, new information tends to come at the end of a clause, and it tends to coincide with the heaviest stress. The writer has used the 'There + be . . .' structure to ensure that the time adverbials come at the end of their clauses, and a reasonable spoken version (with the heaviest stress in capitals) might be:

There are more accidents from NOON to MIDnight than there are in the MORNing.

This new information is then used as given, and summarized in the word 'that'. This 'new-become-given' information is used to initiate the next sentence (the explanation). Another piece of new information is then provided, namely that 'from noon to midnight' coincides with 'the business time'. This again has the final position in the clause, and the heaviest stress on 'business'. So far we have the same kind of structure that we saw in passage (a):

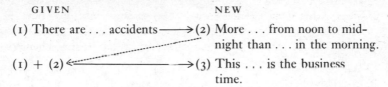

GIVEN   NEW

(1) There are . . . accidents ⟶ (2) More . . . from noon to mid-
                                           night than . . . in the morning.

(1) + (2) ⟵ - - - - - - - - - - ⟶ (3) This . . . is the business
                                           time.

But the next sentence – 'There are quite a number of ac-cidents . . .' – establishes a different pattern to that of (a). The infor-mation introduced in the first two sentences is abandoned. The given information in the third sentence is the same as that in the first – 'There are . . . accidents.' And the time adverbial – 'between 11 and 12pm' occurs at the end of a sentence and is marked by stress, again establishing the points about time as new information. 'This . . .' in the next sentence refers back to the whole set of information asserted in the previous sentence, and functions as given information against which the next new information – the point about drinking and driving – can be introduced. So the 'given – new' pattern of the first two sentences is repeated:

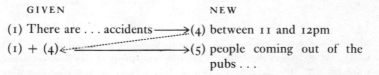

GIVEN   NEW

(1) There are . . . accidents ⟶ (4) between 11 and 12pm
(1) + (4) ⟵ - - - - - - - - - ⟶ (5) people coming out of the
                                           pubs . . .

A similar descriptive analysis of the rest of the passage would show that this pattern is more or less repeated throughout:

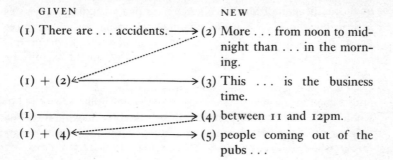

GIVEN   NEW

(1) There are . . . accidents. ⟶ (2) More . . . from noon to mid-
                                           night than . . . in the morn-
                                           ing.

(1) + (2) ⟵ - - - - - - - - - ⟶ (3) This . . . is the business
                                           time.

(1) ⟶ (4) between 11 and 12pm.

(1) + (4) ⟵ - - - - - - - - - ⟶ (5) people coming out of the
                                           pubs . . .

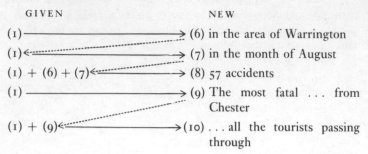

The implications of this contrast are clear. If we wish our students to expand their use of the resources of language we should not ask them to write lists. Learning to use language is not merely a matter of writing correct grammar and expanding your vocabulary. It means, among other things, being able to create texts that utilize to the best advantage what language has to offer. And this is not only an aesthetic matter – the icing on the cake of 'good English' – but a linguistic matter. It cuts right across what language is.

Unity

I have discussed the developmental aspects of the tension that results in the production of a text. Now we must turn to the question of unity; what makes a string of sentences, however they are related thematically, into a *text*? Language has a large number of complex strategies for achieving this unity. I have hinted at how some of them are used in the Ezra Pound poem. But, as we saw, literary usage depends on ordinary language. Our purpose requires a more thorough specification of textual cohesion in ordinary language, since this is the context in which most of our students' writing and speech takes place. Although such a specification is beyond the scope of this book, I shall try to indicate the lines on which it might usefully be made.

One means of achieving cohesion is through *reference*. Pronouns offer a good case, since they usually have to refer back or forwards to a noun phrase to be interpretable. In the 'Savings Scheme' text one pronoun refers outside the text; 'you' refers to the reader and potential customer. There are a very limited number of pronouns in the language, so some repetition is to be expected. As we shall see, repetition is itself a cohesive device. Another type of reference involves demonstratives like 'this', 'that', 'here'. Comparative reference involves a kind of tie between two or more items, so it too is clearly a strong cohesive force. Comparative reference includes items like 'more . . . than . . .', '. . . er than . . .'. In passage (a) some comparative reference is to outside the text; '. . . a much better service' refers to the previous services offered, though no details about them are given. Again, since there are a very limited number of comparative constructions some repetition will inevitably occur. We can see roughly how these reference relations connect items in the text.

I will focus on only three uses of this device in the first passage, and on their effects. The reader may care to work out the effects of other examples. I take the central reference relations in the first passage to be these:

A New Savings Scheme

line			
1	new post office savings scheme . . . which	everybody	post office
2		you . . . you	
3	this savings scheme		
4		you	
5		you . . . you	
6		you . . . your . . . you	
7			us
8			us . . . we
9		you	we
10	a better chance (than this)	you . . . your	we
11			we
12			
13	This . . . a scheme . . . It . . .	you . . . you	

These three sets of references are central because the appeal is trying to set up a relation between 'us', 'you' and the 'new . . . savings scheme'. This three-fold relation, as it is used in the text, represents a basic model of language use:

SPEAKER/WRITER   MESSAGE   LISTENER/READER
    'us'——————→ 'new . . . savings scheme' ——————→ 'you'

Contrast this with 'Accidents in Cheshire'. In this passage there is no sense of this basic communicative structure. The writer has no clear role, and therefore no standpoint from which to approach her writing. No reference is made to any role, except, tentatively, a speculative role – 'That I presume . . .'. Of course, this role can be linguistically and educationally valid, but only when the writer has a communicative framework to develop the theory in. The writer of 'Accidents in Cheshire' was simply told to 'interpret' the facts, so she tries out the role once, finds that it does not work, and abandons it in favour of stating her theories as if they were facts – 'This *is* because of . . .'.

One of the reasons for the writer's failure to construct a cohesive text in this instance shows up in the different projections of readers in the two passages. In the 'Savings Scheme' passage no less than sixteen direct references are made to the projected reader. In 'Accidents in Cheshire' there are none. Yet the repetition of 'you' in 'A New Savings Scheme' is not particularly intrusive. This is partly because some repetition is, as I pointed out, unavoidable in English, but it is also because the 'you' being referred to is *real*. The projected reader wants his money to work for him – 'You will get $7\frac{1}{2}$ per cent . . .', he has medium term interests – '. . . if you are in long enough . . .', and long term interests – '. . . in your later years . . .' and he has children whose interests he wants to protect. Because the writer is able to picture her reader, however roughly, her writing has a direction to go in. 'Accidents in Cheshire' has no such direction. To construct a reader at all we have to abstract from her general style and eliminate more likely possibilities. It is not a newspaper report because it lacks any personal details or central theme. It is not an official report because it is too cursory, and does not offer alternative explanations of the facts. The nearest characterization of the reader would be something like 'teacher/examiner', with the exercise being perceived as a test.

Because the writer is unsure of her role as writer, and has little conception of her intended reader, she cannot formulate a 'message'.

Saying something is difficult if you do not know what you are or who you are talking to. When she was writing 'A New Savings Scheme' she did have a clear idea of these things, and she was able to use it as a reference point. It is for this reason that her final sentences can refer back to her first sentence without any sense of it being contrived. 'Accidents in Cheshire' could not make this kind of reference; the four units comprising the text could be arranged in any order, so there is no first or last sentence.

There are very different patternings of referential items in the two passages. In 'Accidents in Cheshire' reference is limited to within the one- and two-sentence units, reinforcing the cohesion inside these units, but also bringing out the relative lack of cohesion between the units. 'A New Savings Scheme' contains a complex network of relations over the whole passage, whereas the other passage uses these relations only over parts of the passage.

There is a similar patterning with *ellipsis*. Ellipsis involves the omission of words and phrases that have either already been mentioned or may be 'understood' by the reader. English has very complex rules which determine what items may be omitted and when, but a simple example will illustrate the notion adequately if we see a stage-by-stage reduction:

  (i) I'm good at chess, but Bobby's better at chess than I am *at chess*.
 (ii) I'm good at chess, but Bobby's better at chess than I *am*.
(iii) I'm good at chess, but Bobby's better *at chess* than I. (More normally, '. . . than *me*'.)
 (iv) I'm good at chess, but Bobby's better *than me*.
  (v) I'm good *at chess*, but Bobby's better.
 (vi) I'm good, but Bobby's better. (If chess has been the subject of conversation.)

Because ellipsis works by constant reference to what has already been said it is clearly another powerful force in drawing a passage together as a unity.

The differences between the passages come out very clearly if we contrast the patterns of their ellipsis:

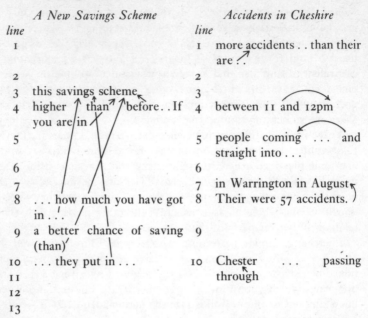

	A New Savings Scheme		Accidents in Cheshire
line		*line*	
1		1	more accidents . . than their are ?.
2		2	
3	this savings scheme	3	
4	higher than before. . If you are in	4	between 11 and 12pm
5		5	people coming . . . and straight into . . .
6		6	
7		7	in Warrington in August
8	. . . how much you have got in . . .	8	Their were 57 accidents.
9	a better chance of saving (than)	9	
10	. . . they put in . . .	10	Chester . . . passing through
11		11	
12			
13			

This contrast seems to provide reasonable evidence that 'A New Savings Scheme' had, in some sense, been conceived as a whole, whereas 'Accidents in Cheshire' had been conceived in relatively closed units. Part of what counts as understanding a text is being able mentally to synthesize the parts into a whole, and this is a skill that is demanded in every school subject. It is true that people can usually understand at a more complex level than they themselves can produce at. But there is still a correlation between understanding and producing. Without first-hand experience of the strategies that can be used to produce a unified text it is difficult for anyone to read such a text and 'get inside' it. We know that letting our students write poetry helps them to understand other people's poems; we know that the use of practical drama enhances students' understanding and enjoyment of plays they see in the theatre. In the same way, practice at creating texts which exploit the language's cohesive resources contributes to a student's ability to make sense of other, perhaps more complex, texts. A unified piece of writing is, in a way, a closed system, and the best way to understand a closed system is from the inside.

The same point also applies to the use of *conjunctions*. The traditional definition of conjunctions only includes items that are in some way equivalent to the 'truth-functional connectives' of formal logic – 'and', 'or', 'implies'. Thus, 'also' and 'but' are roughly equivalent to 'and'; 'so that' is roughly equivalent to 'implies', and so on. It would be difficult to conceive of a text of any length that did not use any of these connectives because logical and causal relationships are so central to our experience, and are therefore central to language itself. In school-subjects students are expected to be able to follow and construct logical and causal connections, sometimes of great complexity. Because there are relatively few of these connectives in English each one must do a multitude of jobs, and students need time and opportunity to discover for themselves the contexts in which they can be used. In spite of the fact that they are so basic to language use, 'Accidents in Cheshire' uses only three of these connectives:

This is *because of* . . .

between 11 *and* 12pm

coming out of the pubs *and* straight into their cars.

This is in spite of the fact that there are abundant opportunities in this kind of writing for establishing logical and causal relations. A piece of persuasive writing like 'A New Savings Scheme' would seem to offer little opportunity for making these connections. But logic must be at the heart of any piece of impelled writing, and in this passage the writer has the demanding logical task of relating her role, her reader and her message at every stage of the composition. Compare the variety and complexity of relations expressed in 'Accidents in Cheshire' with that of this passage:

If (sentence) (sentence)

(Sentence) *so that* (sentence)

(Sentences) *also* (sentence)

(Sentences) *so* (sentence)

For (Noun Phrase) *depending on* (Noun Phrase) (sentence)

For (Noun Phrase) *for* (Noun Phrase) (sentence)

If you did not know that both passages were written by the same person it would be easy to conclude that one writer's language lacked complexity compared to the language of the other writer. It makes sense to compare the complexity of the two passages, but, as I argued in chapter 2, comparison of the complexity of the two language *systems* does not make sense. In this case, both passages originate from the same language system, yet they are very different in quality. I can only conclude once more that we must look not just at the language systems and the language abilities associated with them, but also at the relations between these systems and the tasks they have to do. One of the practical implications of this way of looking at things is that the tasks which most efficiently allow students to explore and develop their language abilities are tasks which are *meaningful*.

We have seen that reference items taken from a small class of words, like pronouns, can result in *repetition* of these items; I quoted the instances of 'you' and 'us/we'. In a sense, repetition is only a special case of reference, since the cohesion that results from repetition depends on the two items both referring, in some sense, to the same thing. However, the wide variety of sub-types of repetition suggests that it should be classified as a separate type of cohesive relation. At its simplest, repetition involves reiteration of the same lexical item (morpheme, word or phrase). There is much more repetition in 'A New Savings Scheme' than in 'Accidents in Chesire', and although repetition is normally considered a stylistic fault, 'A New Savings Scheme' is the stylistically superior. This is partly due to the opportunities each task, as it is perceived by the writer, gives for being linguistically adventurous. If we simply compare a couple of lists of repetitions from each passage then we get no idea of the differences in quality:

A New Savings Scheme		*Accidents in Cheshire*	
line		line	
1	savings	1	accidents
2		2	
3	savings	3	
4		4	accidents
5	savings	5	
6		6	
7	savings	7	accidents
8	save	8	accidents

9		9	accidents
10	savings	10	
11	savings		
12			
13			

The differences emerge if we begin to look at the contexts in which these terms are used:

Contexts of 'savings'		*Context of 'accidents'*	
line		*line*	
1	—— scheme	1	more ——
2		2	
3	—— scheme	3	
4		4	a number of ——
5	a special ——	5	
6		6	
7	—— stamps	7	The most . . . ——
8		8	57 ——
9	a better chance of ——	9	The most fatal ——
10		10	
11	a —— stamp		
12			
13			

In both passages contexts vary, but 'accidents' is only used in contexts to do with quantities, whereas no such simple characterization of the contexts of 'savings' could be made. Because the writer of 'A New Savings Scheme' is concerned with a meaningful language task she must operate at different levels of abstraction, from the relatively concrete level of 'savings stamps' to the more abstract one of 'a special savings'. So the contexts in which she uses her repeated items must vary, because the task demands it. This is a very small example, but when we consider the number of pieces of writing a student must do during eleven years of English lessons then we must acknowledge the cumulative effects of examples like this.

Exploring language is an activity which everyone is engaged upon, and if we were not so dedicated to grading students' writing instead of using it, we would see this more clearly. Exploring language can be as simple as testing out contexts for the word 'savings', or as profound and complex as making a description of an American Indian language from scratch from its two or three remaining speakers. In between there is a rich variety of ways of exploring language.

Take, for example, the writer's use of semantically related terms in the two passages. We are all familiar with exercises of the form, 'Give a synonym for each of these words...', 'Find antonyms for the following...'. In reality, the assumptions made by this kind of exercise are vastly oversimplified as the relations in 'A New Savings Scheme' can show. There are many other semantic relations besides synonymy and antonymy, and all these relations are important. There are several different types of synonymy and antonymy. And all these types and sub-types are explored *in use* by students in their writing. There is, for example, some kind of semantic relationship between 'interest' and '7½ per cent', but 'synonymy' does not describe it. 'Pound' and 'pence' are related, but not by being synonymous. This is not the place to give an exhaustive account of these relations, so I will assume a general understanding of the idea of a relationship of meaning between words. This is quite sufficient to bring out the differences in complexity between the two passages. As part of the composition of 'A New Savings Scheme' the writer has found it necessary to use the notion of *money* at different levels of abstraction and in different manifestations. We find in the passage the following related terms, which I have represented schematically:

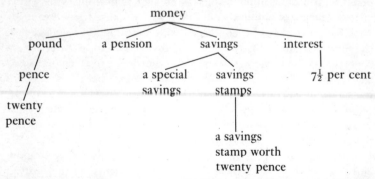

A New Savings Scheme

There is no set of semantic relations in 'Accidents in Cheshire' with anything like this complexity. The nearest is the semantic area of *time*:

Accidents in Cheshire

time

| from noon to midnight | the business time | between 11 and 12pm | the month of August |

The teacher can encourage further exploration of the idea of money because the initial exploration was quite ambitious and there are more relations to work with than in the other passage. Can the writer make her 'special savings' more specific, just as she has given 'savings stamps' as an example of 'savings', and '$7\frac{1}{2}$ per cent' as an example of 'interest'? Can she relate '$7\frac{1}{2}$ per cent' to 'a savings stamp worth twenty pence' for 'every pound'? Can she see that 'a pension' and 'interest' are both forms of *income*? Questions like this do not arise from her exploration of time periods, and it is difficult to see how further exploration could be encouraged on the basis of what she has done.

Relations of reference, ellipsis, conjunction, repetition and meaning are used by every speaker and writer in almost everything they write and say. The analysis and exploration of these ideas is very important and very interesting, but their importance to English teachers lies in their usefulness. For example, can this linguistic technology give us insights into how our students use language and how they perceive their use of language? In my two examples I have tried to show that a systematic analysis of students' work can lead to insights, and can also point to directions for the continuing development of language abilities.

7 Sources

A 'themes' approach and a language approach

English teaching in this country now is in a state of flux. Whether this constitutes confusion or healthy variety depends on your point of view. Certainly every interested group is putting pressure on teachers to adopt *its* aims, methods and ideology. To some employers spelling, punctuation and 'clarity' are the basic language skills, and the interests of this group are reflected in most of the country's examination syllabuses. To many educational theorists a developing awareness of oneself and one's relations to the world should be the primary aim of English teaching, and these attitudes are reflected in some 'experimental' examination syllabuses, like the Mode III C.S.E. and G.C.E. examinations. Changes in the structure of education are making their demands on teaching techniques and teaching materials; there is an increasing need for mixed-ability teaching, for example. And teachers are struggling to take in the enormous amount of specialist literature in the field. Inevitably, from this teachers are beginning to work out strategies which are designed to cope with at least some of these demands.

It is well outside my scope to survey the whole of the English teaching scene, and in any case such a survey would be out of date before it was completed. Instead I want to discuss two important approaches which have developed in the teaching of English, and also to suggest a do-it-yourself framework which teachers may find useful as a starting-point.

The first approach is the so-called 'themes' approach. This is now embodied in scores of textbooks, many of them beautifully presented and imaginatively constructed. The concept is quite simple. Instead of writing essays each week on topics as disparate and unrelated as 'The Advantages and Disadvantages of Television' and 'A Dream', doing comprehensions on out-of-context passages culled from 'The Bedside Guardian' or Alan Sillitoe's novels, classes are given a fairly lengthy period of time to work through some idea or topic in detail. Favourite themes are loneliness, advertising, old age, work. It should go without saying that this approach was not suddenly invented by someone. Good English teachers were using themes and projects as pegs to hang written work and reading on long before the ideas were enshrined in textbooks.

The advantages of this approach are very great. Since many of the textbooks are written by experienced teachers they tend to reflect the interests and ordinary experience of the students pretty well. The structure allows for the use of a wide variety of different language functions, including the use of drama, poetry, debate, discussion, projects as well as the writing of essays of various kinds. Other material, prepared by the class teacher, or even by the students themselves, can be readily integrated with the available material.

This approach has been, and still is being, used with profit in schools and colleges, and it may seem carping to criticize it. It provides an approach, in that it offers material and allows flexible use of teaching methods, but there is implicit in it no guide as to the part language plays in the classroom or in real life. If we take the themes approach to its conclusion then every theme could, in principle, be contracted out to another subject. Many, like old age, men and women and work would fit nicely into a sociology syllabus. Some, like locality or pollution, would go well in an enlightened geography, history or environmental studies syllabus. Even if these topics formed part of a multi-disciplinary syllabus, what is left of the peculiarly *language* perspective? Spelling and punctuation? Language is a vast and complex subject; there must be more to it than that.

One perspective commonly adopted by teachers in using a themes approach is through literature. Many of the best textbooks, using, as they do, poems, extracts from plays and novels, and short stories, lend themselves well to literary responses from students. And many English teachers are trained in literature rather than language, and are therefore profoundly aware of the value of literary response. Moreover, literature, in our society, is one of the main sources for language standards; it is a prestige form of language and provides a measure against which other forms of language can be compared (and against which, unhappily, they can be seen to have failed).

One consequence of tying language study to literature in this way is that it becomes unnecessary for classes to think rationally about language. Much time in English lessons may be spent thinking rationally about the themes provided by textbooks – old age, violence and so on. And in itself there is nothing wrong with this; students need time and opportunities to work out their relations with their society and their world. But very little time may be spent exploring language itself. Every other subject in the curriculum has methods of exploration and ways of thinking proper to itself. A chemistry student performs and watches experiments; but he is also expected to be able to think and reason *about* those experiments. The study of history does not merely consist of describing series of events; you must also be able to relate them as cause and effect, to abstract from them, and to pick out some as more significant than others. But all too often when a class is thinking about language the lowest level of differentiation will do as a conclusion.

As an example, compare extracts from Eric Williams's textbook *People* (1970) and Peter Doughty's (1971) *Language in Use*. *People* uses a themes approach, with a very heavy emphasis on literature, but with many opportunities for a whole variety of responses in speech and writing. It is sympathetic to the students' point of view, without being condescending, and is altogether an excellent example of its type. Yet there is a very blurred focus on how students' speech and writing work; few explicit guidelines are given on how students can reflect on the language they use, and how they can exploit those reflections. *Language in Use* turns this approach inside out. Its themes are specifically concerned with language (see page 104) and it is very careful not only to begin from students' experience of language, but also to use that starting point for exploration of 'the nature of (students') own experience as users of language'. Both books deal at one point with the idea of 'talking for the sake of talking'. Eric Williams begins with a lengthy extract from Harold

Pinter's *The Last To Go* as stimulus material. One of the exercises in 'writing dialogue' is as follows:

> Write a scene like *The Last To Go*, a conversation between two people in one of the following settings:
> (a) at a bus stop
> (b) in a cafe or restaurant while killing time before the waiter arrives
> (c) in a train compartment when the train has stopped
> (d) in a youth club when nothing is happening
> (e) in a doctor's waiting room

Unit J4 'Social talk' in *Language in Use* uses no references to any literary model; it simply asks students

> . . . to prepare short sketches which will show what they think is likely to happen when people are thrown together in a situation where they feel impelled to say something . . . . The situation needs to be a very simple one, like people gathering at a bus stop, or sitting in a train much delayed, or being in the room while a repair is carried out.

However, whereas Eric Williams's exploration stops with the writing (and presumably the acting out) of a dialogue, Peter Doughty uses the resulting sketches as a basis for explicitly examining the pressures and constraints that operate in this kind of talk:

> . . . after watching the sketches, the class should consider such questions as:
> (a) (i) where the audience was limited to one or two . . .
>   (ii) where the audience may be only one person but the context is formal, public or social . . .
>   (iii) where the talk is merely preliminary.
> (b) what subjects are not acceptable?
> (c) what else are we conveying while talking and what are we discovering about other people?

The differences between the approaches are decisive. Eric Williams exploits the literary model presented by Pinter; Peter Doughty exploits the model that students already carry in their heads. Eric Williams finishes when he has a written end-product. For Peter Doughty there is no end-product; there is a use of language which provides a focus for a study of language.

For many of the teachers who are using and learning how to use it
– they include me – *Language in Use* has radically changed attitudes
to language teaching, and indeed to language itself. For readers
unfamiliar with this source I will give a brief outline of its structure,
with an example of one of the units, and examples of the kind of
writing that can emerge from it.

Language in Use is organized into three themes, each of which is
subdivided into three or four sections. Each section is further subdivided into between nine and thirteen units, and each unit contains
material for three or four sessions. The rigorous structure is decep-
tive, however, because the units can be mixed, altered or selected
from according to taste. In more detail the structure is:

Themes	*Sections*	*Units*
(1) Language – its nature and function	(A) Using language to convey information	A1 Words and actions A6 Reporting Parliament . . . . . .
	(B) Using language expressively	B3 Reading the news B7 Fact and fiction . . . . . .
	(C) Sound and Symbol	C4 Accent C10 Spelling . . . . . .
	(D) Pattern in language	D4 Patterns in language D13 Preaching . . . . .
(2) Language and individual man	(E) Language and reality	E3 Reticence E7 'Write me an essay.' . . . . . .
	(F) Language and culture	F3 Tags for people F8 How we use slang . . . . . .
	(G) Language and experience	G2 Watching games G13 Language and art . . . . . .
(3) Language and social man	(H) Language in individual relationships	H1 Family names H7 Pub and club . . . . . .
	(J) Language in social relationships	J3 Crowds J10 Talking on the telephone . . . . . .

(K) Language in social   K3 Negotiating
    organizations   K10 Informing the public
                          . . . . . .

An example of a unit from Language in Use

Language and Art   G13

This unit is concerned with the problems that arise when we want to use language to talk about certain kinds of experience which are essentially non-verbal.

It explores the language used in the discussion of art forms like music, painting, sculpture and design, and examines the special demands that this makes upon the relationship between the writer and his audience.

> A collection of texts will be needed for the particular art form selected. Suitable examples include, for music, sleeve-notes on gramophone records, excerpts from record reviews in *Melody Maker* or *The Gramophone*, notes in concert programmes; and in other arts columns in daily and Sunday newspapers.

---

[1] In this session, the class should become acquainted with a particular kind of writing about one of the arts. Circulate a selection of jazz, pop and classical record-sleeve notes and reviews, for members of the class to make notes on general features of the style for comment and discussion.

The class should look for all the ways in which the writer tries to give the reader an awareness of what he is to hear. Points to consider include:

(*a*) use of metaphor and analogy

(*b*) reference to experience of other senses, such as sound described in terms of touch, or visual patterns described in terms of sound

(*c*) how the writer indicates what a listener's response is likely to be.

[2] In this session the focus should shift to an exploration of what other means writers use to represent in words experience which is essentially non-verbal. Points for study include:

(*a*) what references are made:

(i) to other music by the same group, band or composer

(ii) to other music of the same period

(iii) to other art forms and artists

(*b*) how much knowledge of the form does the writer assume in his reader?

(*c*) how much knowledge of the history of music does he assume?

(*d*) does he expect his reader to be able to follow an argument using the technical language of musical description?

The object is to show that a writer is often driven to assume a great deal of prior experience of the art in his audience if he is to make any sense of the music in words.

[3] This session requires the presentation of a piece of music, chosen by the class. After hearing it they should write a short piece suitable for a magazine or record sleeve. Ask the class to divide into three groups and have each group write for a different audience.

Circulate the drafts and discuss how successfully the class has coped with the problems of finding a verbal equivalent for what it has heard.

The following two pieces of writing were done by students on an 'O'-level course in response to an exploration of language and art which followed roughly the lines of Unit G13 in *Language in Use*. They are about different pieces of music since the writing was not done in class, but the differences in perspective and of relations to audience of the two passages is very clear. Readers are not invited to decide which is 'better', but to ask themselves how these pieces of writing could be used in class to further develop each writer's sense of what audience is being written for and how the style and content of the writing is influenced by this.

Thin Lizzy: *Old Flame* (from Johnny the Fox L.P.)

The song is very sad as the singer remembers a girl he was once, and still is, in love with. The tune and words are simple and uncomplicated, and the music seems to be searching for something. The sad guitars seem to pine for a love now lost.

The singer is sad it is now all over and can still remember the things they did together, he cannot forget her and seems lonely.

When they were together, they were like one, being together all the time. People would watch them and say how much in love they were.

When he was with her, and even when she wasn't with him, his heart was like a fire, burning for her. Although she has now gone, he still has a glowing spark for her that never dies in an eternal pile of glowing ashes.

The song was written as though it really happened to the person and they are putting their own, personal feelings into the song. Because he felt so strongly about the girl he cannot forget her, she is like an eternal glowing ember in a fire. The ember was once a great fire and now he feels lost without the girl, as if a part of him was missing, and all he wants to do is go back to his home although he will never forget the girl, an old flame of his.

Stravinsky: *The Rite of Spring*

The music slowly gently softly begins then proceeds into a virtuosa, racing as water swirling rapidly through a gorge, to come out gently as a spring which trickles down the mountainside.

Suddenly tremendously the music reaches peaks as the river which is ominously threatened, glides as a bird escaping, dancing freely reaches the safety of the lake. Here the music dances happily until once more as water in a whirlpool it rages furiously crazily, threatened by all creation. Until finally as water over a fall it accepts and glides safely harmoniously to a close into peace.

One of the chief disadvantages of approaches to English teaching which do not start from language itself is that they place immediate restrictions on what is to count as suitable material for classroom study. Using literary criteria it would be very difficult to explore the language involved in chatting, or chatting up, or gossiping. Yet these things participate in our language experience no less really than the language of the poem or the novel does. If our classroom study of language is to be true to its subject, and to the experience of our students, then we must be prepared to use any part of the complex field of discourse that makes up our language. *Language in Use* provides a framework which may be filled by almost any of the major areas of language likely to be experienced by students. And it is able to do this because it takes experience of language as its major concern.

The learning principle on which it is based is the sound and all-pervading one of reflexivity. Students are encouraged not only to write and speak but also to consider and analyse what they are doing *in* the acts of speaking and writing. This means using their own speech and writing as text for examination. They are allowed to turn their knowledge of language back into the results of their own language skills and their explicit language knowledge. And again the perspective is linguistic; the emphasis is on making already-existing language skills explicit, then using the resulting awareness to develop the skills still further.

Language in Use is an extremely useful source for English teaching. But it is not without its weaknesses. For example, its authors claim that no knowledge of linguistic techniques is required to use it. But teachers without *some* knowledge about linguistics would find it hard to see where Unit D8 *Marked and unmarked* was leading, or what kind of context Unit D5 *What is a rule?* might fit into. Unit E6 *Colour labels* makes a lot more sense if you have read Godfrey Lienhardt's (1961) *Divinity and Experience* than if you have not. On the other hand, it also shows that there is a sound basis of scholarship behind the units, and that the more familiar a teacher is with the background knowledge, the better he will be able to use the units.

The framework I want to suggest for language study requires skills and knowledge which English teachers are not at present expected to have. However, it allows for any area of language skill or experience to take a legitimate place in the classroom. I suggest that the following three fundamental aims do allow for any area of language to be taken seriously:

(1) Students should develop a respect for their own language.
(2) Students should develop their ability to use language in a variety of different situations.
(3) Students should develop an ability to think rationally about their own language, and about the language of others.

These aims involve three different kinds of intention. The second – the ability to *use* language – has been the central theme of this book.

We may regard this as the basic level: basic in the sense that the
other two aims are realized through it. The next level is thinking
about language. Obviously this cannot be done by someone who is
not already familiar with language, because he would have nothing to
think *about*. And if the first aim – developing a respect for language –
is adopted, it will determine how the other two aims are achieved. It
will mean, for example, that students' errors will not be regarded as
evidence of incompetence, but as means whereby linguistic potential
can be realized. It will mean that teachers will be more careful in
their decisions about whether a student's error *is* really an error
because it differs from the teacher's language system. It means that
areas of students' language that were hitherto educationally out of
bounds will be more accessible to rational discussion.

A model for teaching

Much of this book has been concerned to show that the ability to use
language may be developed in the context of a respect for one's own
language. I want to suggest some possible ways in which a rational
study of language can be achieved with the same perspective.

We may, for convenience, divide the using of language into four
topics for educational purposes, and the thinking about language into
two:

(1) *Using language*	(2) *Thinking about language*
(i) demands	(i) theories
(ii) resources	(ii) reality
(iii) problems	
(iv) solutions	

We may begin by looking first at students' direct language experience
as it is relevant to each topic, then move away to their indirect
experience – what they know and believe about the language experience of their acquaintances, then what they know and believe of the
experience of people not familiar to them.

I believe that these ventures in the exploration of language must
be co-operative. A teacher has only limited access to his students'
language experience, and if he is to discover more about it in order to
teach more efficiently he must be prepared to listen to what his
students say. Furthermore a co-operative approach will allow
students to discover for themselves the need for some classroom

activities instead of having tasks imposed upon them on the basis of the teacher's beliefs about their needs. So I envisage the preliminary work in a scheme like this being carried out by the students *and* the teacher. The scheme I have suggested might look something like this:

(1) *Using language*
  (A) (i) *demands*   What demands are made on students' language resources?
      (ii) *resources* What resources do students have to meet these demands?
      (iii) *problems* Under what circumstances are the resources adequate or inadequate for the demands made?
      (iv) *solutions* What can be done to bridge gaps between resources and demands?
  (B) (i) *demands*   What demands are made on the language resources of other people, particularly adults, known to the students?
      (ii) *resources* What resources do students have to meet these demands?
      (iii) *problems* Under what circumstances are the resources likely to be adequate or inadequate for the demands?
      (iv) *solutions* What can be done to bridge gaps between the students' resources and those demands?
  (C) (i) *demands*   What other demands are likely to be made on students' language resources in the course of their lives?
      (ii) *resources* What resources do students have to meet those demands?
      (iii) *problems* Under what circumstances are the resources likely to prove adequate or inadequate for the demands?
      (iv) *solutions* What can be done to bridge gaps between the students' resources and those demands?

(2) *Thinking about language*
  (A) (i) *theories* What theories and ideas about language do students already have?
      (ii) *reality* How do these theories match the ways students in fact use language?

	(iii) *theories*	What disagreement is there between the theories?
(B)	(i) *theories*	What theories and ideas about language are held by adults known to the students?
	(ii) *reality*	How do these theories match the way these people in fact use language?
	(iii) *theories*	What disagreement is there between the theories?
(C)	(i) *theories*	What theories and ideas about language are held by people not known by the students?
	(ii) *reality*	How do the theories match the way people do in fact use language?
	(iii) *theories*	What disagreement is there between the theories?

This is only a suggested framework, but I think it is realistic, allowing for adaptations made necessary by the complications of practice. In particular it begins with the only logically possible starting point – the language experience of the learner. It is this that provides the key to language study; the material for this study is all around us, if we can only learn how to listen for it.

Further reading

An excellent introduction to current thinking on grammar is Frank Palmer's *Grammar*. He discusses in detail the different ideas of 'grammatical rule', and the more technical terms used in chapter 1, like 'distribution' and 'word class'. He also gives the reader some idea of the main grammatical theories that have been developed in recent decades. There is less discussion of theory in J. M. Sinclair's *A Course in Spoken English: Grammar*, but it provides some effective, practical ways of approaching grammatical description.

On the necessity of understanding your students' language systems William Labov's paper *The Logic of Non-standard English* is essential reading. This is a polemical paper, and Labov argues from a small number of examples, but the case he makes is very convincing. The importance of the relationship between students' and teachers' language systems is a major theme of several of the papers in C. B. Cazden's *Functions of Language in the Classroom*. Dell Hymes' introduction to the book is particularly recommended.

As a grammatical reference book, Randolph Quirk's *A Grammar of Contemporary English* is an essential addition to the school or college library. It is rather expensive to buy yourself, but there is a shorter, and cheaper, version: *A University Grammar of English* by Quirk and

Greenbaum. Quite why the authors wanted to associate the book with universities I am not sure. The larger version is the best and most exhaustive grammatical description of the structure of English speech that there is at the moment.

For readers interested in the sound-structure of English speech, J. D. O'Connor's *Phonetics* should provide an adequate introduction. A. C. Gimson's *An Introduction to the Pronunciation of English* is more advanced, and more detailed on English. Really it is better read in conjunction with a specialized course on phonetics and phonology.

There is a good deal of valuable information about how English spelling works in Kenneth Albrow's *The English Writing System: notes towards a description.*

Geoffrey Leech's *Semantics* is about the most accessible book on modern scientific approaches to meaning. My personal view is that Leech's own perspective tends to colour his discussion of some issues. It is still worth reading, though you will probably find the later chapters difficult to follow. Much more readable is Stephen Ullmann's *Semantics: An Introduction to the Science of Meaning*. It would be unfair to say that it is out of date, but the reader should be aware that a lot has happened in semantics since it was published.

M. A. K. Halliday's *Explorations in the Functions of Language* is definitely the book to read on language functions. It is a bit hard going in parts, but very rewarding. An alternative, and widely adopted, system for describing language function is explained in James Britton's *The Development of Writing Abilities (11–18)*.

The theory on which Chapter 6 is based is elaborated more fully in M. A. K. Halliday and Ruqaiya Hasan's *Cohesion in English*. This is far from being light reading, but is very useful as a reference book.

An excellent review of English teaching methods over recent decades is William B. Currie's *New Directions in Teaching English Language*. Doughty, Pearce and Thornton's *Language in Use* is an essential book for any English teacher, whatever his or her perspective.

Two very good introductory books on linguistics are David Crystal's *Linguistics* and Y. R. Chao's *Language and Symbolic Systems*.

Bibliographical references

ALBROW, K. (1972) *The English Writing System: notes towards a description* (Longman).

BARNES, D. *et al.* (1969) *Language, the Learner and the School* (Penguin).

BRITTON, J. *et al.* (1975) *The Development of Writing Abilities, 11–18* (Macmillan).

BURGESS, C. *et al.* (1973) *Understanding Children Writing* (Penguin).

CAZDEN, C. B. *et al.* (eds) (1972) *Functions of Language in the Classroom* (New York, Teachers College Press).

CHAO, Y. R. (1968) *Language and Symbolic Systems* (Cambridge University Press).

CRYSTAL, D. (1971) *Linguistics* (Penguin).

CURRIE, W. B. (1973) *New Directions in Teaching English Language* (Longman).

DOUGHTY, P., PEARCE, J. and THORNTON, G. (1971) *Language in Use* (Edward Arnold).

DOUGHTY, P. (1973) *Language Study, the Teacher and the Learner* (Edward Arnold).

DOUGHTY, E. A. and DOUGHTY, P. (1974) *Using Language in Use* (Edward Arnold).

GAUSS, C. F. (1801) *Disquisitiones Arithmeticae.* Quoted in Stewart, I. (1975) *Concepts in Modern Mathematics* (Penguin).

GILLAM, C. W. (1960) *Graded English Language Papers for General Certificate O Level* (Harrap).

GIMSON, A. C. (1970) *An Introduction to the Pronunciation of English* (Edward Arnold).

HALLIDAY, M. A. K. (1973) *Explorations in the Functions of Language* (Edward Arnold).

HALLIDAY, M. A. K. and HASAN, R. (1976) *Cohesion in English* (Longman).

HARRIS, Z. S. (1946) From morpheme to utterance. *Language* 22, 3.

HOLT, J. (1973) *Freedom and Beyond* (Penguin).

HYMES, D. (1972) Introduction in Cazden, C. B. (1972).

LABOV, W. (1973) The logic of non-standard English. In Keddie, N., *Tinker, Tailor . . . The Myth of Cultural Deprivation* (Penguin).

LABOV, W. (1973) The linguistic consequences of being a lame. *Language in Society* 2, 1.

LYONS, J. (1968) *Introduction to Theoretical Linguistics* (Cambridge University Press).

LAWTON, D. (1968) *Social Class, Language and Education* (Routledge & Kegan Paul).

LEACH, E. (1964) Anthropological aspects of language: animal categories and verbal abuse. In Lenneberg, Eric H. (ed.) *New Directions in the Study of Language* (Massachusetts Institute of Technology).

LIENHARDT, G. (1961) *Divinity and Experience: The Religion of the Dinka* (Oxford University Press).

LIUBLINSKAYA, A. A. (1957) The development of children's speech and thought. In Swan, B. (ed.) *Psychology in the Soviet Union* (Routledge & Kegan Paul).

O'CONNOR, J. D. (1973) *Phonetics* (Penguin).

PALMER, F. (1971) *Grammar* (Penguin).

POUND, EZRA (1928) *Selected Poems* (Faber).

QUANG PHUC DONG (1969) Quoted in Jackendoff, R. S. *Semantic Interpretation in Generative Grammar* (Massachusetts Institute of Technology).

QUIRK, R. *et al.* (1972) *A Contemporary Grammar of English* (Longman).

QUIRK, R. and GREENBAUM, S. (1973) *A University Grammar of English* (Longman).

ROBINSON, W. P. (1972) *Language and Social Behaviour* (Penguin).

SARTRE, J-P. (1943) *Being and Nothingness*, trans. H. E. Barnes (Methuen).

SINCLAIR, J. M. (1972) *A Course in Spoken English: Grammar* (Oxford University Press).

THOMAS, D. (1952) *Collected Poems 1934–1952* (Aldine Press).

THORNTON, G. (1974) *Language, Experience and School* (Edward Arnold).

TRUDGILL, P. (1975) *Accent, Dialect and the School* (Edward Arnold).

ULLMANN, S. (1962) *Semantics: An Introduction to the Science of Meaning* (Blackwell).

WILLIAMS, E. (1970) *People* (Edward Arnold).

WITTGENSTEIN, L. (1935) *Philosophical Investigations* (Blackwell).

Index